All scripture is from the *Authorized King James Bible*

"A Sequential Chronology Of End Time Events – Expanded Edition," by Don T. Phillips. ISBN 978-1-62137-753-5.

Published 2015 by Virtualbookworm.com Publishing Inc., P.O. Box 9949, College Station, TX 77842, US. ©2015, Don T. Phillips. All rights reserved. No part of this publication may be reproduced, stored in a retrieval system, or transmitted in any form or by any means, electronic, mechanical, recording or otherwise, without the prior written permission of Don T. Phillips.

A Sequential Chronology Of End Time Events

Scriptural Record with Narrative And Cross Reference To

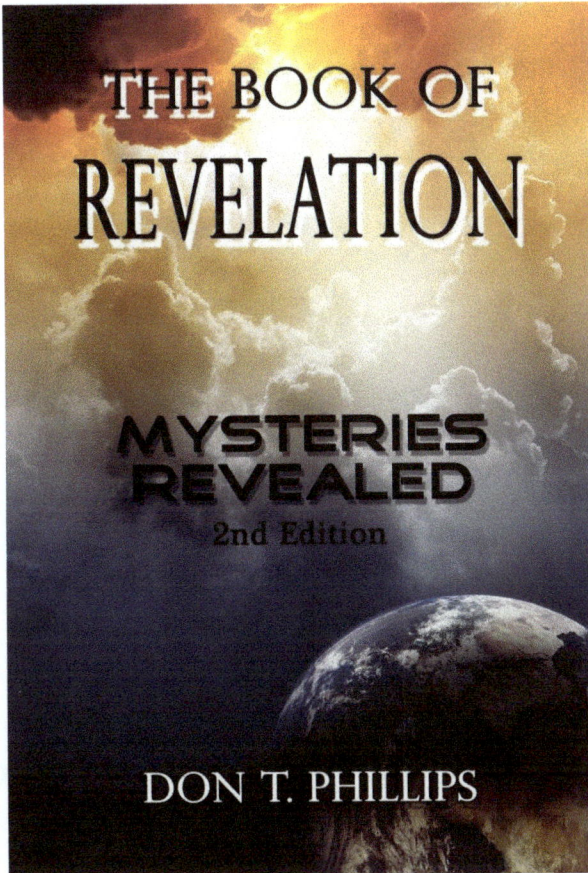

THE BOOK OF REVELATION

MYSTERIES REVEALED

2nd Edition

DON T. PHILLIPS

Don T. Phillips

All scripture is from the *Authorized King James Bible*

"A Sequential Chronology Of End Time Events – Expanded Edition," by Don T. Phillips. ISBN 978-1-62137-753-5.

Table of Contents

A Chronology of End Time Events As Recorded
 In the *Book of Revelation* 1

The Book of Revelation: *Overview* 3

 The 7 Seals 3

 The 7 Trumpet Judgments 4

 The 7 Bowl/Vial Judgments 4

 The Millennial Kingdom and Eternity 5

The Book of Revelation: *Topical Outline* 5

The Book of Revelation In Chronological Order
 Scriptural Record 11

 Prologue and a Salutation 11

 Instructions to John 12

 John Sees the Risen Christ 13

 John's Reaction and the Sovereignty of Jesus Christ 14

 Letters to the 7 Churches 15

 John is Called to Heaven 20

 The Throne of God 23

 The 7 Seal Scroll: Who is Worthy to Open? 25

 Breaking the First 6 Seals 27
  Seals 1-4: Four Horsemen of the Apocalypse 28
  Seal 5: Death of Martyrs 29
  Seal 6: Earth and Heavens Disrupted 30

Seal 7: Silence in Heaven..35

Pre-Tribulation Events 36
   1.0   War in the Heavenlies: The Sun Clothed Woman
         and the Man Child..37
   2.0   Satan and His Angels Cast Down to the Earth.......39
   3.0   Satan Attacks Jerusalem:
         The 1st Jerusalem Campaign 40
   4.0   Rise of the Antichrist 41
   5.0   Rise of the False Prophet 43
   6.0   Mark of the Beast (666) 44
   7.0   The Man Child Identified......................................45
   8.0   The Gospel is Preached Unto All the World.........46
   9.0   The Two Witnesses...47
   10.0   An Announcement: *The Fate of Babylon*..............48
   11.0   Warning about the Mark of the Beast 50

Trumpets 1-4..51

Sealing of the 144,000 53

Trumpet 5 (Woe 1)..55

Trumpet 6 (Woe 2)..56
   Babylon is Destroyed...57
    Religious Babylon is Destroyed 58
    Commercial Babylon is Destroyed 61

The Little Scroll 64
   The Two Witnesses are Slain................................65
   Earthquake Destroys 1/10 of Jerusalem................67

The 3rd Woe Comes Quickly...67

The 7th Trumpet Sounds 68

The Wheat Harvest of All Believers 68
   Rapture of the Saints..69

The Saints in Heaven 69

Rapture of the *Ecclesia*: Exegesis 71

The Bema Seat Judgment..............................75

The Marriage of the Lamb 76

Prelude to the 7 Bowl Judgments........................77

The 7 Bowl Judgments: *The Wrath of God*..............79

The First 5 Bowl Judgments 79

The 6th Bowl Judgment:
The 2nd Jerusalem Campaign......................81

Harvest of the Earth:
The Grape Harvest of All Nonbelievers 82

The 7th Bowl Judgment 84

The 2nd Advent of Christ 85

The Battle of Armageddon............................86

The Winepress of God 86

Fate of the Antichrist and The False Prophet.............87

The Binding of Satan and the Millennial Kingdom 87

Martyrs are Rewarded................................90

End of the 1st Resurrection.............................90

The End of Time as We Know It 91

Satan's Last Battle: *The 3rd Jerusalem Campaign* 91

The White Throne Judgment...........................92

New Heavens and a New Earth.........................93

The Eternal Kingdom of God..........................93

The New Jerusalem...................................94

Gifts to the Resurrected Saints.........................96

Words of Comfort and Warnings.......................97

The Book of Revelation In Chronological Order..........99

Bibliography 145

A Chronology of End Time Events
As Recorded In the
Book of Revelation

The Book of Revelation is not sequential in structure. There are three keys necessary to understanding a correct time-sequenced chronology. The *first key* is to recognize that the 7 seals are not sequentially linked to the 7 trumpets and 7 bowl judgments. The 7 seals provide an overview of conditions and that will exist and several key events which will take place during the Tribulation Period. The *second key* is that the Tribulation period is not 7 years' long, but only 1260 days or about 3.5 years in duration. The 7 bowl judgments are sequentially followed by the 7 Bowl Judgments: Both span the entire Tribulation Period and define a time of great persecution, trial and testing. Finally, the *third key* is to understand that the Book of Revelation compiled by John the revelator is a literary *bifid*. The bifid involves Chapters 9-11 compared to Chapters 12-14. Chapters 9-11 provide a broad description of what happens when the 7 Trumpets sound: Chapters 12-14 give many details of what is happening just prior to the 7 trumpet judgments and during this same period of time. The following graphic depicts the sequential progression in the Book of Revelation with the literary bifid. Other OT books with this structure are Isaiah, Ezekiel, Daniel, and Zechariah.

Prologue	Vision of Christ	Letters to 7 Churches	Vision of God's Throne	The Seven Seal Scroll	The 7 Seals Broken	The Millennial Kingdom	Eternity Begins	Closing Dialog
Rev 1:1-8	Rev 1:9-20	Rev 2-3	Rev 4	Rev 5	Rev 6, 8:1	Rev 20:1-6	Rev 21, 22:1-5	Rev 22:6-20

The Tribulation Period

1260 Days

The Seven Seals	Rev 6, 8:1
Wrath of Satan	Wrath of God
The Seven Trumpets	The Seven Bowls

The Two Witnesses

The Blfed

| Rev 8:8-13 Rev 9:1-21 Rev 11, 15:1 | Rev 12-14 | Rev 15-16 |

The 7th Trumpet

Rapture of Believers	Rev 11:15-19
Bema Seat Judgment	
Believers in Heaven	Rev 7:9-17
Wedding of the Lamb	Rev 19:1-10
The Little Scroll	Rev 10:1-11

| Second Advent of Christ | Rev 19:11-16 |
| Battle of Armageddon | Rev 16:12-16 |

Pre-Tribulation Events

War in Heaven	Rev 12:1-8
Satan Cast to Earth	Rev 12:9-12
Satan Attacks Jerusalem	Rev 12:13-17
The Two Witnesses	Rev 11:1-15
Rise of Antichrist	Rev 13:1-10
Rise of False Prophet	Rev 13:11-15
Mark of Beast (666)	Rev 13:16-18
The Man-Child	Rev 14:1-5
Gosple Preached Throughout World	Rev 14:6-7

| Destruction of Religious Babylon | Rev 17 |
| Destruction of Commercial Babylon | Rev 18 |

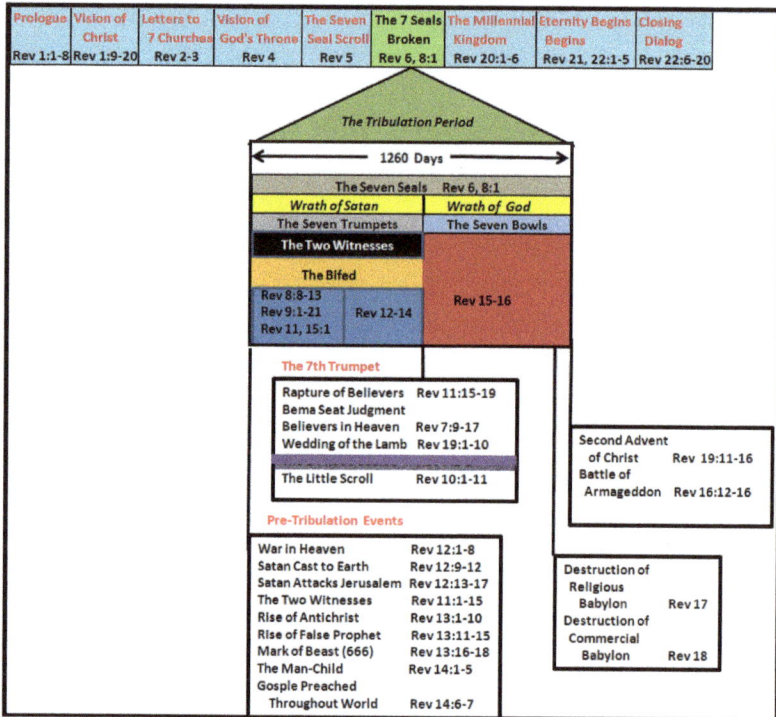

The 7 trumpet judgments bring terrible conditions upon both the earth and mankind, but the 7 bowl judgments bring unprecedented and catastrophic events upon both the earth and mankind. Careful study of the meaning and purpose of the tribulation period will show that the 7 Trumpet judgments parallel the *Wrath of Satan* upon the earth and its inhabitants; while the 7 Bowls or Vials (KJV) are the Wrath of God upon Satan and his followers. In the companion book *Revelation: Mysteries Revealed,* it is shown that the 7 trumpets are sounded over a 1245 day period of time, and the 7 Bowls of God's Wrath are poured out over a short period of time; only 15 days. The total period of tribulation is 1260 days.

The Book of Revelation: *Overview*

- The book begins with a *salutation and Vision of Christ* in Chapter 1.
- Chapters 2 and 3 contain *7 Letters* to *7 Churches.*
- Chapter 4 contains a *Vision of God's Throne in heaven.*
- Chapter 5 is an *interlude*, in which a scroll that contains the Revelation Record is kept by God and opened by Christ.

The 7 Seals

Chapters 6 and 7 are concerned with removing the *7 seals* from the scroll. As each of Seals 1-6 is removed (Chapter 6), conditions that exist during the Tribulation period are revealed. In *Revelation: Mysteries Revealed* (Phillips) it is shown that the Tribulation Period is not 7 years in duration, but 3.5 years/ 1260 days. The Tribulation period of 3.5 years is identical to the period of time during which the *7 trumpet judgments* (Wrath of Satan) take place and the 7 bowls / vials (Wrath of God) are poured out upon Satan and his followers.

- Chapter 7 contains two events which will take place *before* the Wrath of God (the 7 bowls) take place: (1) 144,000 *redeemed Jewish Christians* will be sealed from God's Wrath… they will populate the millennial kingdom. (2) A great multitude is shown in heavens which are the *raptured and resurrected saints.*
- As Chapter 8 begins, the 7th seal is opened and the 3.5 year tribulation period is about to be revealed to John the revelator. The following period of time is so devastating and important to God's plan for the earth that all of heaven is stunned and there is silence for *about half an hour* (Rev 8:1).

- As 7 angels prepare to sound, a remarkable revelation takes place. We are told that the *prayers of all the saints* are kept in heaven before the throne of God. A censer is thrown from earth to heaven and there are thunders, lightnings and an earthquake. The Tribulation period is about to commence (Rev 8:1-6).

The 7 Trumpet Judgments

- Rev 8:1-13, 9:1-21, 11:15-19. The *7 Trumpets sound* sequentially: They span 1250 days of the 1260 day tribulation period.
- The *Rapture* occurs at the Blowing of the 7th Trumpet (Rev 11:15-19), which also initiates the *Wrath of God....* The 7 Bowls.
- The *Wedding of the Lamb* (Jesus Christ) will take place in heaven following the *Bema Seat Judgment* of all believers (Rev 19:1-10).

The 7 Bowl/Vial Judgments

As the Wedding of the Lamb and the Bema Seat Judgment take place in heaven: The Wrath of God is poured out upon the Earth. The pouring out of the *7 Bowls* devastates planet earth and brings unprecedented destruction. The Bowls are poured out between when the 7th Trumpet sounds on The Jewish *Feast of Trumpets* (Tishri 1) and the Jewish *Feast of Atonement/Yom Kippur* on Tishri 10.

- The first 6 vials/bowls are poured out in rapid succession over a 10 day period (Rev 15-16).
- The 7th Bowl (Rev 19:11-21) brings two major events

- o   *Babylon*, the *Commercial and Religious center of Satan* is destroyed (Rev 17-18).
- o   The *2nd Advent of Christ* takes place at the *Battle of Armageddon* (Rev 19: 1-21)

The Millennial Kingdom and Eternity

- *Satan* is bound for 1000 years in the bottomless Pit (Rev 20:1-2)
- The *Antichrist* and the *False Prophet* are thrown into the *Lake of Fire and Brimstone* (Rev 20:1-3)
- The *Martyrs* are rewarded (Rev 20:4-6)
- The 1000 year *Millennial Kingdom* takes place (Rev 20:7-9)
- Satan is released, and the earth is cleansed of him and his followers at the last great battle begin good and evil (Rev 20:10-15)
- The *Great White Throne* judgment takes place (Rev 20:7-15)
- The *Earth* is renovated (Rev 21:1)
- *Eternity* begins (Rev 21:2-27)

The Book of Revelation: *Topical Outline*

This book will list the events which were recorded by the Apostle John in the *chronological order* in which they occur. This chronology is fully explained in **The Book of Revelation:** *Mysteries Revealed*. The complete chronological scriptural record is given with descriptive narratives in **The Book of Revelation:** *Compiled in Chronological Order*. The structure of the entire Book of Revelation as recorded by John is given to John by Christ in Revelation 1:19.

The Biblical record is cross referenced to the 30 Book Chapters by **Red Chapter References.** For example, read the **Preface** and **Overview** sections of **Revelation**: Mysteries Revealed now. The following chronological sequence of events is recorded in the Book of Revelation.

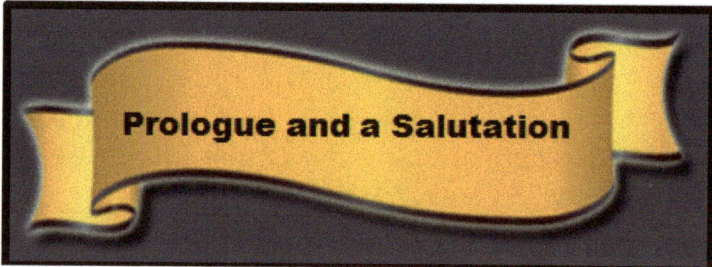

Prologue and a Salutation

*Prologue and a Salutation...... ....*Rev 1:1-8

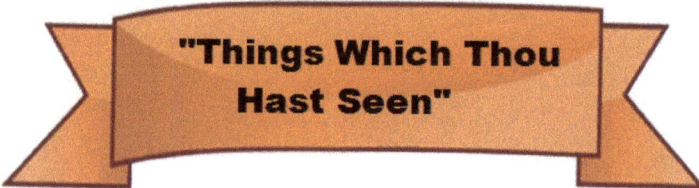

"Things Which Thou Hast Seen"

Instructions to John...............................Rev 1:9-11

John sees the risen Christ.........................Rev 1:12-16

*John's Reaction and the Sovereignty
    Of Jesus Christ..............................*...Rev 1:17-20

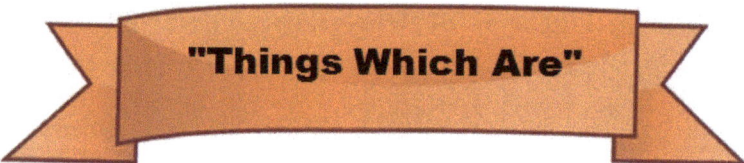

"Things Which Are"

Letters to 7 churches............................Rev 2-3

John is called to heaven........................Rev 4:1-2

The Throne of God...............................Rev 4:3-11

The 7-Sealed Scroll.............................Rev 5:1-14

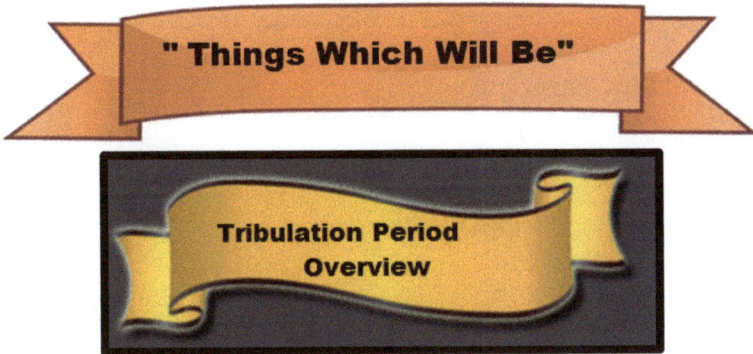

" Things Which Will Be"

Tribulation Period Overview

Opening/Breaking the First 6 Seals

Seals 1-4: 4 Horsemen of the Apocalypse....Rev 6:1-8

Seal 5: Death of Martyrs........................Rev 6:9-11

Seal 6: Earth and Heavens Disrupted.........Rev 6:12-17

Seal 7: Silence in Heaven........................Rev 8:1

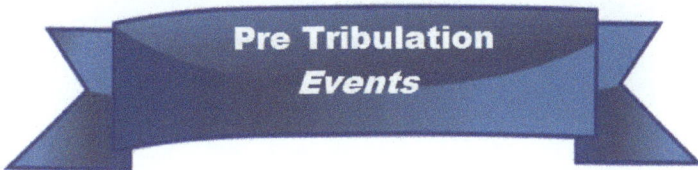

Pre Tribulation Events

War in the Heavenlies: The Sun clothed Woman and the Man Child...................Rev 12:1-8

*Satan and his angels cast
Down to the Earth*..............................Rev 12: 9-12

Satan attacks Jerusalem:
The 1st Jerusalem Campaign.......…...........Rev 12:13-17

Rise of the Antichrist............................…...Rev 13:1-10

Rise of the False Prophet......................…......Rev 13:11-15

Mark of the Beast (666).......................…....Rev 13:16-18

The Man Child Identified…………………......Rev 14:1-5

*The Gospel is Preached Unto
All the World*…………………………......Rev 14:6-7

The Two Witnesses..............................…....Rev 11:1-6

An Announcement: The Fate of Babylon....Rev 14:8

Warning About the Mark of the Beast.......Rev 14:9-13

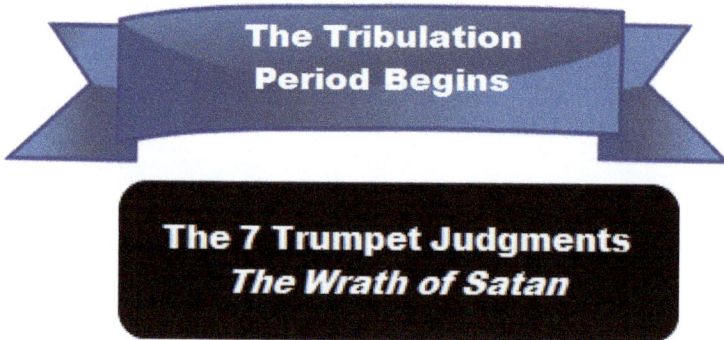

The Tribulation Period Begins

The 7 Trumpet Judgments
The Wrath of Satan

The First 4 Trumpet Judgments……………......Rev 8:2-13

Sealing of the 144,000........................…......Rev 7:1-8

The 5th Trumpet Sounds (Woe 1)............Rev 9:1-12

The 6th trumpet Sounds (Woe 2).............Rev 9:13-21

Babylon is Destroyed.........................Rev 14:8
    Religious Babylon Destroyed...........Rev 17:1-18
    Commercial Babylon Destroyed........Rev 18:1-24

The Little Scroll..............................Rev 10:1-11

The Two Witnesses are Slain...................Rev 11:7-12

Earthquake Destroys 1/10 of Jerusalem....Rev 11:13

The 3rd Woe Comes Quickly..................Rev 11:14

The 7th Trumpet Sounds (Woe 3):
    The Wheat Harvest of All Believers.....Rev 14:14-16
    Rapture of the Saints......................Rev 11:15-19
    The Raptured and Dead Believers in
       Heaven...................................Rev 7:9-17
    The Bema Seat Judgment.................Rev 20:4-6
    The Marriage of the Lamb.................Rev 19:1-10

Prelude to the 7 Bowl Judgments.............Rev 15:1-8

The 7 Bowl Judgments
The Wrath of God

The First 5 Bowl Judgments......................Rev 16:1-11

The 6th Bowl Judgment
    Satan Prepares to Destroy Jerusalem
      The 2nd Jerusalem Campaign...........Rev 16:12-16

The 7th Bowl Judgment............Rev 16:17-21
    The 2nd Advent of Christ.............Rev 19:11-16
    The Battle of Armageddon............Rev 19:17-21

Satan is Bound for 1000 Years............Rev 20:1-3

Martyrs are Rewarded...................Rev 20:4

End of the First Resurrection.............Rev 20:5-6

The End of Time as We Know It..........Rev 20:7

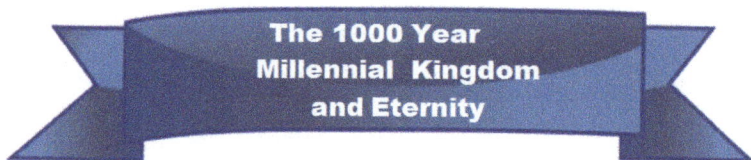

**The 1000 Year
Millennial Kingdom
and Eternity**

Satan's Last Battle:
    The 3rd Jerusalem Campaign............Rev 20:8-10

The White Throne Judgment.............Rev 20:11-15

New Heavens and New Earth............Rev 21:1

The Eternal Kingdom of God.............Rev 21:2-8

The New Jerusalem........................Rev 21:9-27

Gifts to the Resurrected Saints............Rev 22:1-5

Words of Comfort and Warning...........Rev 22:6-21

The Book of Revelation
In
Chronological Order
Scriptural Record

We will now present the Revelation Record from the King James Bible in the Chronological sequence that it occurs, with relevant comments. This Chronology is meant to complement and accompany the book: *Revelation: Mysteries Revealed* by Don T. Phillips.

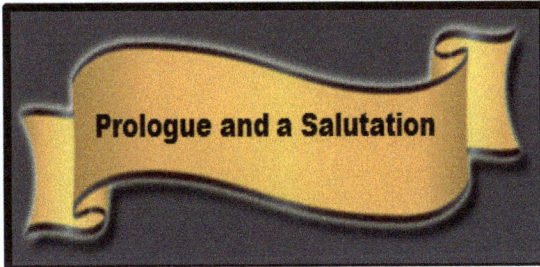

Prologue and a Salutation

Chapter 1

Prologue and a Salutation

John is a Roman political prisoner who has been exiled to the Island of Patmos off the coast of Asia (Minor). He was *in the spirit* praying one day around 93 AD when *God* came to him.

Revelation 1:1-8
[1] The Revelation of Jesus Christ, which God gave unto him, to shew unto his servants things which must shortly come to pass; and he sent and signified it by his angel unto his servant John:
[2] Who bare record of the word of God, and of the

testimony of Jesus Christ, and of all things that he saw.
[3] Blessed is he that readeth, and they that hear the words
of this prophecy, and keep those things which are written
therein: for the time is at hand.
[4] John to the seven churches which are in Asia: Grace be
unto you, and peace, from him which is, and which was,
and which is to come; and from the seven Spirits which are
before his throne;
[5] And from Jesus Christ, who is the faithful witness, and
the first begotten of the dead, and the prince of the kings of
the earth. Unto him that loved us, and washed us from our
sins in his own blood,
[6] And hath made us kings and priests unto God and his
Father; to him be glory and dominion for ever and ever.
Amen.
[7] Behold, he cometh with clouds; and every eye shall see
him, and they also which pierced him: and all kindreds of
the earth shall wail because of him. Even so, Amen.
[8] I am Alpha and Omega, the beginning and the ending,
saith the Lord, which is, and which was, and which is to
come, the Almighty.

Instructions to John

From the context, a period of time…. likely short… would
pass after God addresses John. John is *in the spirit on the
Lord's day* when he hears a *voice like a trumpet* speaking
to him: It is the voice of the resurrected Jesus Christ.

Revelation 1:9-11
[9] I John, who also am your brother, and companion in
tribulation, and in the kingdom and patience of Jesus
Christ, was in the isle that is called Patmos, for the word of

God, and for the testimony of Jesus Christ.
[10] I was in the Spirit on the Lord's day, and heard behind me a great voice, as of a trumpet,
[11] Saying, I am Alpha and Omega, the first and the last: and, What thou seest, write in a book, and send it unto the seven churches which are in Asia; unto Ephesus, and unto Smyrna, and unto Pergamos, and unto Thyatira, and unto Sardis, and unto Philadelphia, and unto Laodicea.

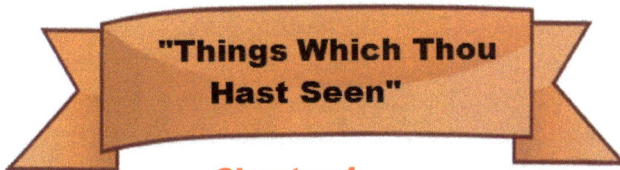

"Things Which Thou Hast Seen"

Chapter 1

John Sees the Risen Christ

John has been told in Rev 1:11 that he was to write *what thou seest; write it in a book;* and *send it to the 7 churches in Asia.* As John hears this voice, he turned to see our Lord Jesus Christ in all of His heavenly glory.

Revelation 1:12-16
[12] And I turned to see the voice that spake with me. And being turned, I saw seven golden candlesticks;
[13] And in the midst of the seven candlesticks one like unto the Son of man, clothed with a garment down to the foot, and girt about the paps with a golden girdle.
[14] His head and his hairs were white like wool, as white as snow; and his eyes were as a flame of fire;
[15] And his feet like unto fine brass, as if they burned in a furnace; and his voice as the sound of many waters.
[16] And he had in his right hand seven stars: and out of

his mouth went a sharp twoedged sword: and his
countenance was as the sun shineth in his strength.

John's Reaction and the Sovereignty of Jesus Christ

John is overwhelmed when he sees the risen Christ, and he falls at His feet as if he was dead. The majesty of Christ in this instance has been painted by many great artists, but no combination of artist, paints and brush can capture the majesty of our lord and savior. Seeing John's reaction, Christ addresses Him and us; *fear not.* Every Christian should fall upon their knees at this statement. We may go through ridicule, rejection, trials and tribulation… but Christ assures us… *fear not.* There is no fear in living for Jesus Christ and following after Him.

Revelation 1: 17-20
[17] And when I saw him, I fell at his feet as dead. And he laid his right hand upon me, saying unto me, Fear not; I am the first and the last:
[18] I am he that liveth, and was dead; and, behold, I am alive for evermore, Amen; and have the keys of hell and of death.
[19] Write the things which thou hast seen, and the things which are, and the things which shall be hereafter;
[20] The mystery of the seven stars which thou sawest in my right hand, and the seven golden candlesticks. The seven stars are the angels of the seven churches: and the seven candlesticks which thou sawest are the seven churches.

Letters to the 7 Churches

The apostle John is again instructed to write down what he has seen, what he will now be told about 7 churches, and the visions that he will be shown. John repeatedly assures us that he actually *saw* what was going to take place far into the future. For now, he must faithfully record what Christ tells him about the 7 churches in Asia (Asia Minor). As far as we know, each of these churches was founded by the Apostle Paul. They were all very active in John's day and represented a cross section of churches even today. These letters should be carefully studied by every pastor and church leader today. Christ includes in each letter what he liked about the church, and what he hated in each church. The things of which Christ approved and disapproved are thae same today as almost 2000 years ago. *He who has an ear to hear, let him hear.*

Revelation 2:1-29
*[1] Unto the angel of the church of **Ephesus** write; These things saith he that holdeth the seven stars in his right hand, who walketh in the midst of the seven golden candlesticks;*
[2] I know thy works, and thy labour, and thy patience, and how thou canst not bear them which are evil: and thou hast tried them which say they are apostles, and are not, and hast found them liars:
[3] And hast borne, and hast patience, and for my name's sake hast laboured, and hast not fainted.
[4] Nevertheless I have somewhat against thee, because thou hast left thy first love.
[5] Remember therefore from whence thou art fallen, and

repent, and do the first works; or else I will come unto thee quickly, and will remove thy candlestick out of his place, except thou repent.

[6] But this thou hast, that thou hatest the deeds of the Nicolaitans, which I also hate.

[7] He that hath an ear, let him hear what the Spirit saith unto the churches; To him that overcometh will I give to eat of the tree of life, which is in the midst of the paradise of God.

*[8] And unto the angel of the church in **Smyrna** write; These things saith the first and the last, which was dead, and is alive;*

[9] I know thy works, and tribulation, and poverty, (but thou art rich) and I know the blasphemy of them which say they are Jews, and are not, but are the synagogue of Satan.

[10] Fear none of those things which thou shalt suffer: behold, the devil shall cast some of you into prison, that ye may be tried; and ye shall have tribulation ten days: be thou faithful unto death, and I will give thee a crown of life.

[11] He that hath an ear, let him hear what the Spirit saith unto the churches; He that overcometh shall not be hurt of the second death.

*[12] And to the angel of the church in **Pergamos** write; These things saith he which hath the sharp sword with two edges;*

[13] I know thy works, and where thou dwellest, even where Satan's seat is: and thou holdest fast my name, and hast not denied my faith, even in those days wherein Antipas was my faithful martyr, who was slain among you, where Satan dwelleth.

[14] But I have a few things against thee, because thou hast there them that hold the doctrine of Balaam, who taught Balac to cast a stumblingblock before the children of Israel, to eat things sacrificed unto idols, and to commit fornication.

[15] So hast thou also them that hold the doctrine of the

Nicolaitans, which thing I hate.

[16] Repent; or else I will come unto thee quickly, and will fight against them with the sword of my mouth.

[17] He that hath an ear, let him hear what the Spirit saith unto the churches; To him that overcometh will I give to eat of the hidden manna, and will give him a white stone, and in the stone a new name written, which no man knoweth saving he that receiveth it.

*[18] And unto the angel of the church in **Thyatira** write; These things saith the Son of God, who hath his eyes like unto a flame of fire, and his feet are like fine brass;*

[19] I know thy works, and charity, and service, and faith, and thy patience, and thy works; and the last to be more than the first.

[20] Notwithstanding I have a few things against thee, because thou sufferest that woman Jezebel, which calleth herself a prophetess, to teach and to seduce my servants to commit fornication, and to eat things sacrificed unto idols.

[21] And I gave her space to repent of her fornication; and she repented not.

[22] Behold, I will cast her into a bed, and them that commit adultery with her into great tribulation, except they repent of their deeds.

[23] And I will kill her children with death; and all the churches shall know that I am he which searcheth the reins and hearts: and I will give unto every one of you according to your works.

[24] But unto you I say, and unto the rest in Thyatira, as many as have not this doctrine, and which have not known the depths of Satan, as they speak; I will put upon you none other burden.

[25] But that which ye have already hold fast till I come.

[26] And he that overcometh, and keepeth my works unto the end, to him will I give power over the nations:

[27] And he shall rule them with a rod of iron; as the vessels of a potter shall they be broken to shivers: even as I

17

received of my Father.

[28] And I will give him the morning star.

*[29] He that hath an ear, let him hear what the Spirit saith
unto the churches.*

Revelation 3:1-22

*[1] And unto the angel of the church in **Sardis** write; These
things saith he that hath the seven Spirits of God, and the
seven stars; I know thy works, that thou hast a name that
thou livest, and art dead.*

*[2] Be watchful, and strengthen the things which remain,
that are ready to die: for I have not found thy works perfect
before God.*

*[3] Remember therefore how thou hast received and heard,
and hold fast, and repent. If therefore thou shalt not watch,
I will come on thee as a thief, and thou shalt not know what
hour I will come upon thee.*

*[4] Thou hast a few names even in Sardis which have not
defiled their garments; and they shall walk with me in
white: for they are worthy.*

*[5] He that overcometh, the same shall be clothed in white
raiment; and I will not blot out his name out of the book of
life, but I will confess his name before my Father, and
before his angels.*

*[6] He that hath an ear, let him hear what the Spirit saith
unto the churches.*

*[7] And to the angel of the church in **Philadelphia** write;
These things saith he that is holy, he that is true, he that
hath the key of David, he that openeth, and no man
shutteth; and shutteth, and no man openeth;*

*[8] I know thy works: behold, I have set before thee an
open door, and no man can shut it: for thou hast a little*

strength, and hast kept my word, and hast not denied my name.

[9] Behold, I will make them of the synagogue of Satan, which say they are Jews, and are not, but do lie; behold, I will make them to come and worship before thy feet, and to know that I have loved thee.

[10] Because thou hast kept the word of my patience, I also will keep thee from the hour of temptation, which shall come upon all the world, to try them that dwell upon the earth.

[11] Behold, I come quickly: hold that fast which thou hast, that no man take thy crown.

[12] Him that overcometh will I make a pillar in the temple of my God, and he shall go no more out: and I will write upon him the name of my God, and the name of the city of my God, which is new Jerusalem, which cometh down out of heaven from my God: and I will write upon him my new name.

[13] He that hath an ear, let him hear what the Spirit saith unto the churches.

*[14] And unto the angel of the church of the **Laodiceans** write; These things saith the Amen, the faithful and true witness, the beginning of the creation of God;*

[15] I know thy works, that thou art neither cold nor hot: I would thou wert cold or hot.

[16] So then because thou art lukewarm, and neither cold nor hot, I will spue thee out of my mouth.

[17] Because thou sayest, I am rich, and increased with goods, and have need of nothing; and knowest not that thou art wretched, and miserable, and poor, and blind, and naked:

[18] I counsel thee to buy of me gold tried in the fire, that

thou mayest be rich; and white raiment, that thou mayest be clothed, and that the shame of thy nakedness do not appear; and anoint thine eyes with eyesalve, that thou mayest see.

[19] As many as I love, I rebuke and chasten: be zealous therefore, and repent.

[20] Behold, I stand at the door, and knock: if any man hear my voice, and open the door, I will come in to him, and will sup with him, and he with me.

[21] To him that overcometh will I grant to sit with me in my throne, even as I also overcame, and am set down with my Father in his throne.

[22] He that hath an ear, let him hear what the Spirit saith unto the churches.

John is Called to Heaven
Chapter 3, Chapter 23

Revelation 4:1-2
[1] After this I looked, and, behold, a door was opened in heaven: and the first voice which I heard was as it were of a trumpet talking with me; which said, Come up hither, and I will shew thee things which must be hereafter.
[2] And immediately I was in the spirit: and, behold, a throne was set in heaven, and one sat on the throne.

The Apostle John is called into heaven before the throne of God. In this Chapter we see a rare glimpse of where God sits upon His throne. In addition to beholding God in all of His glory, John is introduced to 24 elders and 4 living creatures (beasts) who praise God continuously. It is crucial to recognize that traditional pre-tribulation rapture

20

theologians all point to Revelation 4:1 as when the church is raptured out. These teachers ignore two fundamental facts: (1) the *first* is the failure to recognize that Christ never promised any Christian that they would not experience persecution and tribulation. In fact, Paul specifically taught the following truth.

> *[3b] We glory in tribulations also: knowing that tribulation worketh patience;*
> *[4] And patience, experience; and experience, hope:*
> *[5] And hope maketh not ashamed; because the love of God is shed abroad in our hearts by the Holy Ghost which is given unto us.   Romans 5:3-5*

Those who follow after Christ either before or during the Tribulation period should expect to be persecuted for their faith. (2) The second mistake that all pre-tribulation rapturists make is to recognize that while Christians are not exempt from tribulation, they are promised that they will not experience the Wrath of God; which are the 7 bowl judgments. (3) The third mistake is to recognize why John was called to heaven in Revelation 4:1. He is called to heaven to be shown and record what will happen on earth and in heaven as the tribulation period occurs at the end of this age. Note that although the vast majority of all prophecy teachers identify this with the rapture described by Paul in I Thessalonians 4:13-18 and I Corinthians 15:50-54, when John is called to heaven in Rev 4:1 any identification with the rapture of living believers living and the resurrection of the righteous dead fails to meet logic and scriptural scrutiny.

- John is not preceded by any of the dead in Christ as Paul revealed
- John did not receive a new eternal, non-corruptible body
- John was not called forth by angels to meet Christ in the air, he was taken directly to the throne room of God
- John was not called to heaven by the *sound of a trumpet*, but by a *voice* that *resembled a trumpet*
- John was not judged for his eternal rewards, nor did he stand before the Bema Seat
- When the 7th trumpet sounds… the last in a series of 7 trumpets that sound… John later sees and writes down what is unmistakably the Rapture of all saints; living and dead (Rev 11:15:19).

How has the misinterpretation that this is a pre-tribulation rapture been taught and propagated for so long? The answer lies in a failure to carefully compare scripture to scripture, and an erroneous belief that all Christians must be removed from the earth before a 7 year tribulation period begins. Such teachings have no basis whatsoever in God's Holy Word. Christ Himself taught that the harvest of the earth would not occur until *after* the tribulation period is over (7 trumpets) but before the Wrath of God comes upon the earth (7 bowls).

> *[29] Immediately **after** the tribulation of those days shall the sun be darkened, and the moon shall not give her light, and the stars shall fall from heaven, and the powers of the heavens shall be shaken:*
> *[30] And **then** shall appear the sign of the Son of man in heaven: and then shall all the tribes of the earth mourn, and they shall see the Son of man coming in the clouds of heaven with power and*

great glory.
[31] And he shall send his angels with a great
sound of a trumpet, *and they* **shall gather together**
his elect *from the four winds, from one end of*
heaven to the other   Matthew 24:29-31

Revelation 4:1 is *exactly what it appears to be*. John is taken up to heaven for only one purpose: To write down the revelation record as he sees future events unfolding before his very eyes. Finally, except for the purpose of why John is taken up to heaven, there is no theological difference in this event and when Paul was taken up to heaven over 50 years earlier (II Corinthians 12:2). When Paul was carried away to heaven, he was told not to reveal what he had seen. When John was taken up to heaven, he was commanded to faithfully write down what he would see. All pretribulation theology is based upon an erroneous interpretation of Rev 4:1 and should be rejected. In *Revelation: Mysteries Revealed* it is persuasively argued based upon scripture that a *Pre-Wrath* rapture is the correct theology.

The Throne of God   Chapter 3

After John is called into heaven, he is immediately taken before the throne of God. He sees incredible things not fully revealed to man before. God is seen seated upon a beautiful throne, surrounded by 24 elders and 4 living creatures (*Zoa: Plural of the Greek word Zoon, which means living one*). This is a unique and wonderful revelation to John. Once before, about 50 years earlier, the Apostle Paul spoke of a *man* (who was Paul) that was caught up into the 3rd heaven which is where God sits upon His throne. However, Paul was not allowed to reveal what he saw. He only wrote that he saw *incredible things*. Here we are given a rare glimpse into the throne room of God.

23

Revelation 4:3-11

[3] And he that sat was to look upon like a jasper and a sardine stone: and there was a rainbow round about the throne, in sight like unto an emerald.

[4] And round about the throne were four and twenty seats: and upon the seats I saw four and twenty elders sitting, clothed in white raiment; and they had on their heads crowns of gold.

[5] And out of the throne proceeded lightnings and thunderings and voices: and there were seven lamps of fire burning before the throne, which are the seven Spirits of God.

[6] And before the throne there was a sea of glass like unto crystal: and in the midst of the throne, and round about the throne, were four beasts full of eyes before and behind.

[7] And the first beast was like a lion, and the second beast like a calf, and the third beast had a face as a man, and the fourth beast was like a flying eagle.

[8] And the four beasts had each of them six wings about him; and they were full of eyes within: and they rest not day and night, saying, Holy, holy, holy, Lord God Almighty, which was, and is, and is to come.

[9] And when those beasts give glory and honour and thanks to him that sat on the throne, who liveth for ever and ever,

[10] The four and twenty elders fall down before him that sat on the throne, and worship him that liveth for ever and ever, and cast their crowns before the throne, saying,

[11] Thou art worthy, O Lord, to receive glory and honour and power: for thou hast created all things, and for thy pleasure they are and were created.

The 7 Seal Scroll: Who is Worthy to Open?
Chapter 4

John's attention now turns to God, who he sees setting on His throne. He holds in His right hand a *book* which is better translated a *scroll.* This is evidently a record of what will shortly come to pass in what we call the *Tribulation Period*, the *1000 year millennial kingdom*, and the *preparation for eternity.* This document is so important that God inquires: *who is worthy to open the scroll?* The 4 creatures on the corner of God's throne; the 24 elders; the host of angels which attend to God; and no man in heaven or the earth can answer the call. John, in his mortal weakness weeps. But suddenly one of the elders declares *weep not; Christ is worthy* to reveal the contents of the scroll. Every creature in heaven now praises the Son of God. John will be able to fulfill his destiny.

Revelation 5:1-14
[1] And I saw in the right hand of him that sat on the throne a book written within and on the backside, sealed with seven seals.
[2] And I saw a strong angel proclaiming with a loud voice, Who is worthy to open the book, and to loose the seals thereof?
[3] And no man in heaven, nor in earth, neither under the earth, was able to open the book, neither to look thereon.
[4] And I wept much, because no man was found worthy to open and to read the book, neither to look thereon.
[5] And one of the elders saith unto me, Weep not: behold, the Lion of the tribe of Juda, the Root of David, hath prevailed to open the book, and to loose the seven seals thereof.
[6] And I beheld, and, lo, in the midst of the throne and of the four beasts, and in the midst of the elders, stood a Lamb as it had been slain, having seven horns and seven eyes,

which are the seven Spirits of God sent forth into all the earth.

[7] And he came and took the book out of the right hand of him that sat upon the throne.

[8] And when he had taken the book, the four beasts and four and twenty elders fell down before the Lamb, having every one of them harps, and golden vials full of odours, which are the prayers of saints.

[9] And they sung a new song, saying, Thou art worthy to take the book, and to open the seals thereof: for thou wast slain, and hast redeemed us to God by thy blood out of every kindred, and tongue, and people, and nation;

[10] And hast made us unto our God kings and priests: and we shall reign on the earth.

[11] And I beheld, and I heard the voice of many angels round about the throne and the beasts and the elders: and the number of them was ten thousand times ten thousand, and thousands of thousands;

[12] Saying with a loud voice, Worthy is the Lamb that was slain to receive power, and riches, and wisdom, and strength, and honour, and glory, and blessing.

[13] And every creature which is in heaven, and on the earth, and under the earth, and such as are in the sea, and all that are in them, heard I saying, Blessing, and honour, and glory, and power, be unto him that sitteth upon the throne, and unto the Lamb for ever and ever.

[14] And the four beasts said, Amen. And the four and twenty elders fell down and worshipped him that liveth for ever and ever.

" Things Which Will Be"

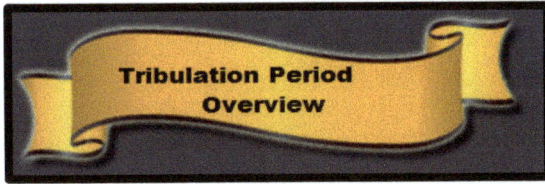

Breaking the First 6 Seals
  Chapters 10 and 11

God has given the scroll to the only one worthy to open it and reveal the contents: our *Lord Jesus Christ*. The scroll is sealed with 7 seals. The scroll cannot be opened until Jesus breaks each seal one by one. It was common practice in the Roman Empire to record important information on papyrus scrolls, and to seal the contents with a wax seal. Most scrolls were secured with only one seal, some with 2 or 3. A seven sealed scroll would be very rare. It is important to realize that the *Revelation Record of the tribulation period* is inside the scroll. Once opened, its contents will reveal what must take place as the 1260 day Tribulation Period runs its course. As Christ breaks seals 1-5, John is shown visions of general conditions that will exist throughout the tribulation period. As seal 6 is broken, John is shown the heavens and earth breaking apart causing massive damage to the earth. The devastation is so severe that *every mountain and every island is moved out of place*. Such a devastating event would logically take place well into the tribulation period. This is strong evidence that the seals describe conditions which span the entire tribulation of 1260 days. As Christ breaks the 7th seal, the anticipation and significance of what will occur during the tribulation period is so awesome that heaven sits in stunned silence for *about one hour* of time.

Seals 1-4: Four Horsemen of the Apocalypse

As Seals 1-4 are broken, John sees imagery which reveals general conditions that will exist as Satan and his followers bring the *Wrath of Satan* upon the earth.

Seal 1: Deception
Seal 2: Wars
Seal 3: Famine
Seal 4: Death

The first 4 seals spawn imagery of 4 supernatural and spiritual beings riding out on four horses of different colors. These are called the *Four Horsemen of the Apocalypse.*

Revelation 6:1-8

*[1] And I saw when the Lamb opened **one of the seals**, and I heard, as it were the noise of thunder, one of the four beasts saying, Come and see.*
[2] And I saw, and behold a white horse: and he that sat on him had a bow; and a crown was given unto him: and he went forth conquering, and to conquer.
*[3] And when he had opened the **second seal**, I heard the second beast say, Come and see.*
[4] And there went out another horse that was red: and power was given to him that sat thereon to take peace from the earth, and that they should kill one another: and there was given unto him a great sword.
*[5] And when he had opened the **third seal**, I heard the third beast say, Come and see. And I beheld, and lo a black horse; and he that sat on him had a pair of balances in his hand.*
[6] And I heard a voice in the midst of the four beasts say, A measure of wheat for a penny, and three measures of

barley for a penny; and see thou hurt not the oil and the wine.
*[7] And when he had opened the **fourth seal**, I heard the voice of the fourth beast say, Come and see.*
[8] And I looked, and behold a pale horse: and his name that sat on him was Death, and Hell followed with him. And power was given unto them over the fourth part of the earth, to kill with sword, and with hunger, and with death, and with the beasts of the earth.

Seal 5: Death of Martyrs   Chapter 28

Seal 5 represents a special type of death that will occur throughout the Tribulation Period. If anyone refuses to take the mark of the beast (666) and refuses to worship the satanic indwelled Antichrist; that person will be *martyred*, likely by guillotined execution. There will be millions of Christians and Jews killed during the Tribulation years. Clearly, followers of Jesus Christ will be slain from the first day that Satan is cast down to the earth until he is defeated at the Battle of Armageddon and removed from the earth. Certainly, Christians will be martyred from when Christ was crucified on the Cross of Calvary until the tribulation period will have run its course. The Christians that will be martyred by Satan and his followers during the tribulation period appear to have a special fate. They seem to be waiting under the Throne of God for the 2nd advent of Christ: They long for retribution and justice.

Revelation 6:9-11
*[9] And when he had opened the **fifth seal**, I saw under the altar the souls of them that were slain for the word of God, and for the testimony which they held:*
[10] And they cried with a loud voice, saying, How long, O Lord, holy and true, dost thou not judge and avenge our blood on them that dwell on the earth?

[11] And white robes were given unto every one of them; and it was said unto them, that they should rest yet for a little season, until their fellow servants also and their brethren, that should be killed as they were, should be fulfilled.

Seal 6: Earth and Heavens Disrupted Chapter 10

The 6th seal predicts that during the Tribulation Period there will be cosmic and earthly disturbances unprecedented in the history of mankind.

Revelation 6:12-17
*[12] And I beheld when he had opened the **sixth seal**, and, lo, there was a great earthquake; and the sun became black as sackcloth of hair, and the moon became as blood;*
[13] And the stars of heaven fell unto the earth, even as a fig tree casteth her untimely figs, when she is shaken of a mighty wind.
[14] And the heaven departed as a scroll when it is rolled together; and every mountain and island were moved out of their places.
[15] And the kings of the earth, and the great men, and the rich men, and the chief captains, and the mighty men, and every bondman, and every free man, hid themselves in the dens and in the rocks of the mountains;
[16] And said to the mountains and rocks, Fall on us, and hide us from the face of him that sitteth on the throne, and from the wrath of the Lamb:
[17] For the great day of his wrath is come; and who shall be able to stand?

These disturbances fulfill the end-time prophecies of Joel.

Joel 2:30-32

> [30] *And I will shew wonders in the heavens and in the earth, blood, and fire, and pillars of smoke.*
> [31] *The sun shall be turned into darkness, and the moon into blood, before the great and the terrible day of the LORD come.*
> [32] *And it shall come to pass, that whosoever shall call on*
> *the name of the LORD shall be delivered: for in mount Zion and in Jerusalem shall be deliverance, as the LORD hath said, and in the remnant whom the LORD shall call.*

The 6th seal also announces that the *great day of His wrath has come*. There is no reason to assume that this day of wrath is anything but a single day: It is the great day of the 2nd Advent of Christ, when the Battle of Armageddon will take place outside of Jerusalem. This *day of wrath* will be immediately preceded by the devastating 7 Bowl/vial judgments which are clearly identified as the *Wrath of God* (Rev 15:7, 16:1). This is not a general condition that persists throughout the last 1260 days of the Church age, but a specific point in time yet future. Note again the important conclusion that the predictions of the 7 seals are partitioned into three different parts. *Seals 1-4* describe general conditions which will exist throughout the entire period of tribulation: they are the direct result of the *Wrath of Satan,* the Antichrist and the False Prophet. We will later discuss these two evil personalities in some detail. The *5th seal* predicts that many Christians will be martyred for their faith during the Tribulation period (Revelation 12:13-17). When the *6th seal* is broken, it announces that the *Day of God's Wrath* has come. This is the great day of the *2nd advent of Christ*, in which He will defeat Satan and all of his forces at the Battle of Armageddon (Rev 19:11-21).

This is the last event of the tribulation period, and should not be confused with either the Wrath of Satan or the Wrath of God. The Wrath of Satan takes place as the 7 trumpets are blown; The Wrath of God is released upon the forces of evil when the 7 Bowls/vials are poured out (Rev 15:1, 15:7, 16:1 and 14:19). These multiple scriptural references leave no doubt that the Wrath of God is poured out with the 7 Bowls... and not before. To summarize:

- Seal 1...... Deception and conquering
- Seal 2...... War and Death
- Seal 3....... Famine and Poverty
- Seal 4....... Death followed by Hades
- Seal 5....... Martyrs and martyrdom
- Seal 6...... Earthquakes, moon and sun blackened, sky rolls up like a scroll; *All* Mountains and islands are moved out of place.

There are most certainly cosmic disturbances and earthquakes which occur throughout the entire sequence of Trumpets and Bowls (Rev 8:5, Rev 11:13, Rev 11:19, Rev 12:16, Rev 16:18), but clearly there will be only *one* point in time at which *every island and every mountain* will be moved out of its place. Can we find when this amazing event occurs? The answer is, YES. This will occur when the 7th Bowl is poured out at the end of this age (Rev 16:20): Right where it should occur. Hence, this is a strong confirmation that the first 6 seals predict events which will occur across the entire tribulation period.

We now again state the important conclusion that the tribulation period is composed of: (1) The 7 Trumpet judgments (*Wrath of Satan* against the earth, Christians and all the Jews) and (2) The 7 Bowl judgments (*Wrath of God* against Satan, the Antichrist, the False Prophet and all unbelievers).

Note also that when the 6th seal is broken mankind is predicted to *hide in fear* in caves and among rocks. Why? ...... *Because the Great Day of his Wrath is come* (Rev 6:17). Contrary to popular interpretation, we identify this *Great Day of Wrath* as a *single day*: it is the *Battle of Armageddon* that will take place after the 7th Bowl is poured out upon the earth. Here again, conjecture becomes near certainty: as each of the first 5 seals are broken general events are described which will occur over the last 1260 days. The lone exceptions to the 6-seal revelation of general conditions seem to be the prediction that *every mountain and island* will be moved out of its place. This clearly will not happen but one time, and logically very near the end of this age and the tribulation period. The second specific prediction when the 6th seal is broken is that the Day of God's Wrath will end the tribulation period: This is the decisive Battle of Armageddon.

Finally, note that there are many prophecy teachers who adamantly teach that the events in the Book of Revelation have all come to pass. ***Really !!*** Challenge anyone who teaches this theology to identify any point in time since the death of Christ in which all mountains and islands have been moved out of place: *They cannot.*

The 7th and final seal is about to be broken, and the Wrath of God (7 Bowls) are about to be poured out upon all the earth's inhabitants (Rev 16:1). Two things are evident. (1) If the Wrath of God will only fall upon unbelievers, the saints (church) must be removed from the earth before the 7 bowl judgments occur; for we are promised that if anyone believes upon the Lord Jesus Christ as their savior, they will not experience God's Wrath. The removal of all who believe upon the Lord Jesus Christ is clearly the long awaited *Rapture of the Saints.* (2) God made a promise to

Abraham almost 6,000 years ago that his seed would inherit the Promised Land. This promise has not been completely fulfilled in the history of Israel. The Old Testament reveals that living Jews will inherit all of the land promised to them, and then they will live upon the land. King David will return to reign over them; and living conditions will be joyous. The land will once again produce figs, grapes and grain in plenty.

These inhabitants of the land must be those 144,000 from the 12 tribes of Israel who have turned to Christ as their long awaited Messiah (Rev 7:1-8), and who are still alive when the Millennial Kingdom begins. This will require that these believers survive the Wrath of God... but how? They will be divinely sealed and protected from the 7 bowl judgments! This divinely ordained protection must happen *after* the 7th Trumpet sounds and *before* the 1st Bowl is poured out.

After the 6th seal is broken, John sees and records this happening in a vision. Remember that as each of the 7 seals is removed, John is shown conditions or events which will later take place as the contents of the scroll are shown to John. Between when the 6th and 7th seals are broken, John is shown how 144,000 Israelites, 12,000 from each of 12 tribes of Israel, are divinely sealed and ordained to live in the Promised Land during the Millennial Kingdom. Each sealed Jewish convert will be supernaturally protected from the 7 bowl judgments (Wrath of God); just as all the other believers in Jesus Christ will be spared by the rapture. The distinction and choice of the 144,000 who will be sealed and inherit the earth for 1000 years is not revealed.

As previously indicated, the first event which must occur between when the 7th trumpet sounds and the 1st bowl is poured out is the removal from the earth of all who have accepted Christ as their savior (except the sealed 144,000). This is the *great multitude that no man can number* (Rev 7:9) They are seen standing before the throne of God in heaven (Rev 7:1,15) who have accepted Jesus Christ as their savior and will escape from the Wrath of God in the *Rapture*. They have emerged out of the Great Tribulation (Rev 7:14).

Chronologically, the sealing of the 144,000 and the raet multitude seen standing before the throne of God are predicted and described after the 6th seal is removed: but both will not happen for another 1245 days. Since Rev 7:1-17 is out of order with a sequential revelation record, we will not present the scriptures which are recorded by John between when the 6th and 7th seals are broken. They will be presented later when we sequentially reach where they actually occur.

Seal 7: Silence in Heaven   Chapters 10 & 11

When the 7th seal is removed (broken) by Christ the contents of the scroll can now be revealed. Specific events which will take place during the 1260 day Tribulation Period will be shown to the Apostle John. The terminal event at the end of this period of time is the 2nd Advent of Christ. It is worth briefly noting that the rapture will take place on Tishri 1: *The Feast of Trumpets*. The Battle of Armageddon will take place on Tishri 10: *The Feast of Atonement* or Yom Kippur (Chapter 9).

This period of time has been awaited for almost 2000 years by the body of Christ. Indeed: *The whole of creation longs for His glorious appearance* (Romans 8:22). While the end of the age and the second advent of Jesus Christ will be a glorious day, it will be preceded by death, destruction and famine. Millions of Christians will die a violent death for their faith. Is there one seminal event which will trigger this period of tribulation, death and famine? *Yes there is….* There will be a great war in heaven which will set all these things in motion (Chapter 14). Heaven is stunned and becomes silent as the 7th seal is broken. The contents of the scroll is about to be revealed.

Revelation 8:1
[1] And when he had opened the seventh seal, there was silence in heaven about the space of half an hour.

Pre Tribulation Events

Pre-Tribulation Events

The 7 seals have been removed by Jesus Christ, and John is about to be shown what will take place during the 1260 days of tribulation. This period of time will unleash the *Wrath of Satan* (7 Trumpet Judgments) upon all believers who are on the earth and the *Wrath of God* (7 Bowl Judgments) upon all unbelievers. The *Rapture* of all believers will take place when the 7th trumpet sounds. Before John writes the revelation record describing this period of time, he is shown an incredible and astonishing war in heaven which will *precede* the Wrath of Satan. This great conflict and its conclusion are recorded by John the revelator in Revelation Chapters 12-14.

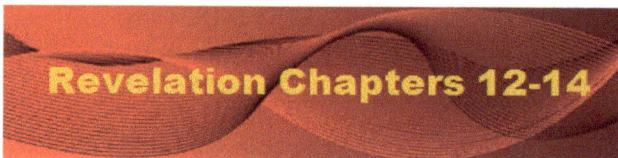

Revelation Chapters 12-14

The 12th – 14th Chapters in the Book of Revelation are perhaps the most difficult to interpret and understand in the entire Book of Revelation. The following 10 events are described in these chapters. They either *precede* the 1260 day Tribulation period, or they are initiated just as the tribulation period begins. They explain what must take place before Satan begins his 1260 day assault on all Jews and Christians.

1.0 *War in the Heavenlies: The Sun Clothed Woman and the Man Child*
2.0 *Satan and his Angels Cast Down to the Earth*
3.0 *Satan attacks Jerusalem:*
    The 1st Jerusalem Campaign
4.0 *Rise of the Antichrist*
5.0 *Rise of the False Prophet*
6.0 *Mark of the Beast* (666)
7.0 *The Man-Child Identified*
8.0 *The Gospel is Preached Unto All the World*
9.0 *The Two Witnesses Arise*
10.0 *Announcements and Warnings*

1.0 War in the Heavenlies:
The Sun Clothed Woman and the Man Child
Chapter 14

There is a great war in heaven between Satan and his angels, and Michael and his angels. This heavenly conflict is beyond human comprehension. Christians are always aware of the *spiritual* conflict between Christians and Satan, but this is a *physical* conflict. The duration of this heavenly war is not given, but it could take some time. In the Book of Daniel, Daniel prayed to god for wisdom and understanding and God sent His angel Gabriel to Daniel. However, it took Gabriel 21 days to reach Daniel because a mighty fallen angel called the *Prince of Persia* fought against him coming to Daniel (Daniel 10:13).

This great heavenly conflict is triggered by the appearance of a *beautiful sun-clothed woman* who is *travailing in birth* and about to *deliver a man-child*. Satan is waiting to destroy this man-child as soon as it is born. It is clear that this man-child is being berthed upon the earth, and just as it is delivered, this man-child is **caught up unto God and unto His throne.** Who is this man-child? The answer to this critical question cannot be completely answered here, but it is addressed in Chapter 14. It can be noted that this man-child is definitely not the baby Jesus Christ as is usually taught. This interpretation requires that the woman is Mary, the man-child is Jesus, and the dragon must be King Herod. This interpretation is so far-fetched; it is hardly worth consideration and is completely debunked in Chapter 14. A much more believable scenario is that the woman is the true church composed of all who believe upon Jesus Christ as their Lord and Savior. The sun which clothes the woman is the radiance and glory of Christ. The moon is the apostate theology of the world… It only reflects spiritual truth in convoluted forms and has no truth at all. The dragon is Satan, who is clearly identified in Rev 12:9. The man-child is a part of the woman, and is berthed from the woman. Careful scriptural study will reveal this man-child as a group of sold-out Christians called *overcomers*, who are apart in each of the 7 churches addressed earlier. They have overcome the world, and having started as a *child; but* they have matured and emerged as a *man*.

Revelation 12:1-8
[1] And there appeared a great wonder in heaven; a woman clothed with the sun, and the moon under her feet, and upon her head a crown of twelve stars:
[2] And she being with child cried, travailing in birth, and

pained to be delivered.

[3] And there appeared another wonder in heaven; and behold a great red dragon, having seven heads and ten horns, and seven crowns upon his heads.

[4] And his tail drew the third part of the stars of heaven, and did cast them to the earth: and the dragon stood before the woman which was ready to be delivered, for to devour her child as soon as it was born.

[5] And she brought forth a man child, who was to rule all nations with a rod of iron: and her child was caught up unto God, and to his throne.

[6] And the woman fled into the wilderness, where she hath a place prepared of God, that they should feed her there a thousand two hundred and threescore days.

[7] And there was war in heaven: Michael and his angels fought against the dragon; and the dragon fought and his angels,

[8] And prevailed not; neither was their place found any more in heaven.

2.0   Satan and His Angels Cast Down to the Earth
Chapter 14

Michael and his angels prevail, and Satan is cast out of heaven down to the earth with his angels. This is the event which all Christians await. Satan is now allowed to enter into the very presence of God and accuse the brethren. He is now defeated and is confined to this earth… he and all of his fallen angels. Satan knows that the end is near, and he has only a short time (1260 days). He now turns upon all Christians and Jews to eradicate them or force them to worship him as God.

Revelation 12: 9-12

[9] And the great dragon was cast out, that old serpent, called the Devil, and Satan, which deceiveth the whole world: he was cast out into the earth, and his angels were cast out with him.

[10] And I heard a loud voice saying in heaven, Now is come salvation, and strength, and the kingdom of our God, and the power of his Christ: for the accuser of our brethren is cast down, which accused them before our God day and night.

[11] And they overcame him by the blood of the Lamb, and by the word of their testimony; and they loved not their lives unto the death.

[12] Therefore rejoice, ye heavens, and ye that dwell in them. Woe to the inhabiters of the earth and of the seal for the devil is come down unto you, having great wrath, because he knoweth that he hath but a short time.

3.0 Satan Attacks Jerusalem:
The 1ˢᵗ Jerusalem Campaign
Chapter 26, Chapter 14

As soon as Satan is cast out of heaven he immediately turns upon the Jewish nation and the people of Jerusalem. He attacks Jerusalem with his fallen angels, and seeks to kill and persecute as many Jews and Christians as possible. This group that Satan pursues is also a part of the Sun Clothed Woman shown in Rev 12:1. In a supernatural and symbolic vision, John sees the *woman* quickly flee Jerusalem. We are told that *she* flees into the *wilderness* where a place has been prepared for her; protected for a *time, times and a half a time* (Rev 12:14). In Rev 12:4 we are told that god would protect and feed this remnant for 1260 days. Comparing scripture to scripture, *times, time and half a time* is equivalent to *1260 days.* Since this protection is against Satan, it also reveals to us how long

40

Satan will be on the earth before he is defeated at the Battle of Armageddon. This defines the true tribulation period.

The serpent (Satan) cast out a *flood* described as *water* to destroy those who are fleeing. But God causes an earthquake to occur which *helps* (saves) them.

Revelation 12:13-17
[13] And when the dragon saw that he was cast unto the earth, he persecuted the woman which brought forth the man child.
[14] And to the woman were given two wings of a great eagle, that she might fly into the wilderness, into her place, where she is nourished for a time, and times, and half a time, from the face of the serpent.
[15] And the serpent cast out of his mouth water as a flood after the woman, that he might cause her to be carried away of the flood.
[16] And the earth helped the woman, and the earth opened her mouth, and swallowed up the flood which the dragon cast out of his mouth.
[17] And the dragon was wroth with the woman, and went to make war with the remnant of her seed, which keep the commandments of God, and have the testimony of Jesus Christ.

4.0 Rise of the Antichrist
Chapter 18, Chapter 17

When God miraculously saves those who are fleeing Jerusalem, Lucifer is *wroth* with anger (Rev 12:17) and now turns on all Christians. The first thing that he will do is to cause a great world leader who has unified all of Europe under his rule to be *wounded to death* by a *sword* or knife (Rev 13:3-4, 12-14). This man's body will then be completely taken over and controlled by Satan…. His name will be the *Antichrist*. This name is not found in the Book of Revelation, but carefully examining I John 2:18, 22 and I John 4:3 the identity of this *beast out of the sea* (of humanity) is made certain.

Revelation 13:1-10

[1] And I stood upon the sand of the sea, and saw a beast rise up out of the sea, having seven heads and ten horns, and upon his horns ten crowns, and upon his heads the name of blasphemy.
[2] And the beast which I saw was like unto a leopard, and his feet were as the feet of a bear, and his mouth as the mouth of a lion: and the dragon gave him his power, and his seat, and great authority.
[3] And I saw one of his heads as it were wounded to death; and his deadly wound was healed: and all the world wondered after the beast.
[4] And they worshipped the dragon which gave power unto the beast: and they worshipped the beast, saying, Who is like unto the beast? who is able to make war with him?
[5] And there was given unto him a mouth speaking great things and blasphemies; and power was given unto him to continue forty and two months.
[6] And he opened his mouth in blasphemy against God, to blaspheme his name, and his tabernacle, and them that dwell in heaven.
[7] And it was given unto him to make war with the saints, and to overcome them: and power was given him over all kindreds, and tongues, and nations.
[8] And all that dwell upon the earth shall worship him, whose names are not written in the book of life of the Lamb slain from the foundation of the world.
[9] If any man have an ear, let him hear.
[10] He that leadeth into captivity shall go into captivity: he that killeth with the sword must be killed with the sword. Here is the patience and the faith of the saints.

5.0 Rise of the False Prophet
Chapter 17

The Antichrist has arisen to make war against all the Jews and against all believers. Satan desires and commands all people to worship him and him alone. To spearhead this effort, he now causes a false prophet to arise who will establish a one-world, apostate, religious system. Note that Satan, the Antichrist and the False Prophet (the Unholy Trinity) mimic and attempt to replace God, Christ and the Holy Spirit (The Holy Trinity). Satan has always wanted to be worshipped and replace God.

Revelation 13:11-15
[11] And I beheld another beast coming up out of the earth; and he had two horns like a lamb, and he spake as a dragon.
[12] And he exerciseth all the power of the first beast before him, and causeth the earth and them which dwell therein to worship the first beast, whose deadly wound was healed.
[13] And he doeth great wonders, so that he maketh fire come down from heaven on the earth in the sight of men,
[14] And deceiveth them that dwell on the earth by the means of those miracles which he had power to do in the sight of the beast; saying to them that dwell on the earth, that they should make an image to the beast, which had the wound by a sword, and did live.
[15] And he had power to give life unto the image of the beast, that the image of the beast should both speak, and cause that as many as would not worship the image of the beast should be killed.

6.0   Mark of the Beast (666)
Chapter 17, Chapter 18

The False Prophet will set up an image that will speak and perform miracles in the rebuilt Herod's Temple in Jerusalem (Daniel 12:11. The image will demand that all who appear before it will bow down and worship Satan and the antichrist. Christ also warned that this image would be set up in the temple in Mat 24:15. Christ called this image the *Abomination of Desolation*. This is a confirmation of Dan 9:27 when this image was revealed in prophecy to Daniel over 1500 years before Jesus delivered the Olivet Discourse. Failure to worship the image will result in death. While the penalty for worshipping Satan and the Antichrist is a horrible death, this is only physical death. For those who capitulate and take the *Mark of the Beast* (666) there will be eternal punishment in the *Lake of Fire*. This is the *second death* (Rev 20:11-15).

Dan 12:11 also reveals that from when this image is set up to the final end of the Antichrist is 1290 days. Note that this is 30 days longer than the actual reign of Satan and the Antichrist. This extra 30 days has been debated by many biblical scholars. It is evidently the time required to judge Satan, his followers and all the nations (Mat 25:31-46) following the Battle of Armageddon.

Revelation 13:16-18
[16] And he causeth all, both small and great, rich and poor, free and bond, to receive a mark in their right hand, or in their foreheads:
[17] And that no man might buy or sell, save he that had the mark, or the name of the beast, or the number of his

name.

[18] Here is wisdom. Let him that hath understanding count the number of the beast: for it is the number of a man; and his number is Six hundred threescore and six.

7.0   The Man Child Identified
Chapter 14

After the Antichrist and False prophet arises, John presents to us what might be the most difficult passage in the entire Book of Revelation: Certainly one of the least understood among prophecy teachers. John now sees 144,000 people standing on Mt. Zion. The question is as follows: Is this the heavenly Mt. Zion or the Earthly Mt. Zion? Christ (the Lamb of God) is shown standing with these 144,000. If this is on the earth, as most claim, this scene must be *after* the 2nd advent of Christ and the Battle of Armageddon, which immediately follows the 7th bowl judgment of God's Wrath. However, the scriptures offer strong evidence that this scene occurs *before* Satan delivers his wrath upon the earth and takes place on the *Heavenly* Mt. Zion.

> *[22] But ye are come unto mount Sion, and unto the city of the living God, the **heavenly** Jerusalem, and to an innumerable company of angels*   Hebrews 12:22

Rev 14:3 reveals that this 144,000 is standing *before the 4 beasts*, the *24 elders of God*, and before the *throne of God*. Conjecture now becomes near certainty… this scene is in *heaven*. The 144,000 are clearly identified in Rev 14:4: they are *redeemed from **among** men*, and they are a *firstfruits harvest*… not from the general resurrection and rapture at the 7th trump. If these 144,000 are not from the general resurrection or rapture of the saints, where did they come from?? The answer is found in Rev 12 5. Just before the Great War in Heaven occurs, a *man-child* is **caught up unto God and unto His throne.** We believe that the scriptures clearly identify this man-child as the 144,000 seen in Rev 14:1-5. They are taken away to heaven *before* the tribulation period begins, and are the same number as the 144,000 Jews who are later sealed from the Bowl judgments. They are **identical to the overcomers** identified in each of the 7 Churches. Here are fully matured adults (typed as a man) who have come to Christ in simple, child-like faith (a man-child) and completely sold out to Christ. They are the overcomers from each of the 7 churches in Revelation 2-3.

Revelation 14:1-5

[1] And I looked, and, lo, a Lamb stood on the mount Sion, and with him an hundred forty and four thousand, having his Father's name written in their foreheads.
[2] And I heard a voice from heaven, as the voice of many waters, and as the voice of a great thunder: and I heard the voice of harpers harping with their harps:
[3] And they sung as it were a new song before the throne, and before the four beasts, and the elders: and no man could learn that song but the hundred and forty and four thousand, which were redeemed from the earth.
[4] These are they which were not defiled with women; for they are virgins. These are they which follow the Lamb whithersoever he goeth. These were redeemed from among men, being the firstfruits unto God and to the Lamb.
[5] And in their mouth was found no guile: for they are without fault before the throne of God.

8.0   The Gospel is Preached Unto All the World
Chapter 19

Christ had told His disciples in Matthew 24:

*And this gospel of the kingdom shall be preached
in all the world for a witness unto all nations; and
then shall the end come.   Matthew 24:14*

Revelation 14:6-7 is the fulfillment of that prophecy. An
angel appears to John's sight flying in the heavens. The
angel is warning every *nation, kindred, tongue and people*
that *judgment* is quickly coming.

Revelation 14:6-7
*[6] And I saw another angel fly in the midst of heaven,
having the everlasting gospel to preach unto them that
dwell on the earth, and to every nation, and kindred, and
tongue, and people,
[7] Saying with a loud voice, Fear God, and give glory to
him; for the hour of his judgment is come: and worship him
that made heaven, and earth, and the sea, and the fountains
of waters.*

9.0   The Two Witnesses
Chapter 13

Concurrent with Satan desecrating the temple in Jerusalem,
God provides two witnesses who will testify during the 3.5
years that the earth is persecuted by Satan, the Antichrist
and the False Prophet (Rev 11: 1-13). We can assume that
they stand and testify in the desecrated temple, because just
before they start their witnessing (Rev 11:3) John is told to
measure the temple of God and its altar (Rev 11:1-2). After
fulfilling their mission, both are slain and lie dead in the
street for 3.5 days (Rev 11:7-9). They are then called to
heaven in a cloud (Rev 11:12). Comparing Matthew 24:30
with Rev 19:11-16 and Rev 11:12: we suggest that they are
raised from the dead at the rapture with all of the other

righteous dead to meet Christ in the air. This will occur as the 7th trumpet sounds. However, we merely conjecture; the scriptures are silent as to exactly when they are raised.

Revelation 11:1-6

[1] And there was given me a reed like unto a rod: and the angel stood, saying, Rise, and measure the temple of God, and the altar, and them that worship therein.

[2] But the court which is without the temple leave out, and measure it not; for it is given unto the Gentiles: and the holy city shall they tread under foot forty and two months.

[3] And I will give power unto my two witnesses, and they shall prophesy a thousand two hundred and threescore days, clothed in sackcloth.

[4] These are the two olive trees, and the two candlesticks standing before the God of the earth.

[5] And if any man will hurt them, fire proceedeth out of their mouth, and devoureth their enemies: and if any man will hurt them, he must in this manner be killed.

[6] These have power to shut heaven, that it rain not in the days of their prophecy: and have power over waters to turn them to blood, and to smite the earth with all plagues, as often as they will.

10.0 An Announcement: The Fate of Babylon
Chapter 18

Revelation 14:8

[8] And there followed another angel, saying, Babylon is fallen, is fallen, that great city, because she made all nations drink of the wine of the wrath of her fornication.

Satan will establish his capital city in a place called *Babylon.* Babylon will be the seat of power for both the

48

Antichrist and the False Prophet. In a short period of time, it will become the commercial and religious center of the world. The location of Babylon is not known, but various Revelation scholars have proposed Rome, Jerusalem and even New York City. In this author's opinion, it is none of these. The Bible mentions Babylon over two hundred and eighty times, and many of those references are to a future city. The name Babylon is likely derived from the ancient city of Babel that was founded by Nimrod. Babel was a wicked and apostate city where a tower was built which reached to the heavens. Nimrod wanted to be worshipped above all other men. God destroyed Babel just as He will the end-time city of Babylon. Babylon was later the city where Nebuchadnezzar ruled over the Babylonian Empire, which conquered the Southern Kingdom of Judah and took all of Israel into a 70 year exile.

Babylon will rise again in the end times, and will be the center of ungodly religion, government, and economics. The ancient city of Babylon was in Iraq, and it is believed that it will once again be rebuilt in Iraq. There is no reason to believe that Christ would conceal or clothe in mystery this city called Babylon which will arise in the end times. Finally, it will not take long for the end-time city of Babylon to become a worldwide center of commerce and trade. However, it is likely that it will take some time to rebuild. A sign that the tribulation period is near will be the rise of a great commercial center called *Babylon*. *He who has eyes, let him see.*

As the tribulation period begins, John is told the final fate of this wicked city. Babylon will be completely destroyed.

This is described in detail as the tribulation period ends in Rev 17-18.

11.0 Warning about the Mark of the Beast

In Rev 13 a warning was issued: If anyone worships the image which will stand in the rebuilt Jerusalem temple that person will be doomed to eternal damnation in the Lake of Fire. This is such an important message that it is repeated in Rev 14:9-13.

Revelation 14:9-13

[9] And the third angel followed them, saying with a loud voice, If any man worship the beast and his image, and receive his mark in his forehead, or in his hand,
[10] The same shall drink of the wine of the wrath of God, which is poured out without mixture into the cup of his indignation; and he shall be tormented with fire and brimstone in the presence of the holy angels, and in the presence of the Lamb:
[11] And the smoke of their torment ascendeth up for ever and ever: and they have no rest day nor night, who worship the beast and his image, and whosoever receiveth the mark of his name.
[12] Here is the patience of the saints: here are they that keep the commandments of God, and the faith of Jesus.
[13] And I heard a voice from heaven saying unto me, Write, Blessed are the dead which die in the Lord from henceforth: Yea, saith the Spirit, that they may rest from their labours; and their works do follow them.

Pre-tribulation events that must occur have been shown to John, and warnings have been issued to all believers. It is now time for Satan to rule and reign for 1260 days. The tribulation period will now begin.

The 7 Trumpet Judgments
The Wrath of Satan

Trumpets 1-4   Chapters 10 & 11

The Tribulation period of 3.5 years duration is now revealed to John, and it begins with the sounding of the 1st of 7 trumpets. It is not stated in John's revelation, but since the Rapture of the Saints takes place when the 7th trumpet sounds, the previous 6 trumpets are likely not sounded in a short period of time but over the 1260 day period of time. Devastation is rained upon the earth as the first 4 trumpets sound. They are often called the *Judgments of Thirds*. The first trumpet causes 1/3 of all the trees and green grass to be burned up. The 2nd trumpet is likely caused by a large meteorite striking one of the oceans: 1/3 of all sea creatures are destroyed and 1/3 of all the ships are destroyed, likely by a tidal wave. The 3rd trumpet is causes a large heavenly body, likely a comet, to strike the earth. This *star* is called *Wormwood* and polluted 1/3 of all fresh water; making it bitter. The 4th trumpet sounds and 1/3 of the sun, moon and stars are darkened. This has been predicted at the opening of the 6th seal and fulfills the prophecy of   Joel 30:32.

Revelation 8:2-13

*[2] And I saw the seven angels which stood before God; and to them were given **seven trumpets**.*
[3] And another angel came and stood at the altar, having a golden censer; and there was given unto him much incense, that he should offer it with the prayers of all saints upon the golden altar which was before the throne.
[4] And the smoke of the incense, which came with the prayers of the saints, ascended up before God out of the

angel's hand.

[5] And the angel took the censer, and filled it with fire of the altar, and cast it into the earth: and there were voices, and thunderings, and lightnings, and an earthquake.

[6] And the seven angels which had the seven trumpets prepared themselves to sound.

*[7] The **first angel sounded**, and there followed hail and fire mingled with blood, and they were cast upon the earth: and the third part of trees was burnt up, and all green grass was burnt up.*

*[8] And the **second angel sounded**, and as it were a great mountain burning with fire was cast into the sea: and the third part of the sea became blood;*

[9] And the third part of the creatures which were in the sea, and had life, died; and the third part of the ships were destroyed.

*[10] And the **third angel sounded**, and there fell a great star from heaven, burning as it were a lamp, and it fell upon the third part of the rivers, and upon the fountains of waters;*

[11] And the name of the star is called Wormwood: and the third part of the waters became wormwood; and many men died of the waters, because they were made bitter.

*[12] And the **fourth angel sounded**, and the third part of the sun was smitten, and the third part of the moon, and the third part of the stars; so as the third part of them was darkened, and the day shone not for a third part of it, and the night likewise.*

[13] And I beheld, and heard an angel flying through the midst of heaven, saying with a loud voice, Woe, woe, woe, to the inhabiters of the earth by reason of the other voices of the trumpet of the three angels, which are yet to sound!

Trumpets 5-7 bring particularly devastating effects upon mankind. They are called *the three woes*.

Before the 5th trumpet sounds, there are 144,000 redeemed Jews sealed in their forehead from 12 tribes of Israel. All 144,000 have accepted Christ as their long awaited Messiah.

Sealing of the 144,000   **Chapter 15**

Recall that John was previously shown a preview of how 144,000 converted Jews were sealed from wrath; between when the 6th and 7th seals were broken (see Revelation 9:4). Remember that as the 6 seals were opened, John is shown conditions and events that will take place as the tribulation period of 1260 days unfold. The 144,000 are sealed no later than when the 5th trumpet sounds (See Revelation 9:4).

In Rev 7:1-8 John was shown 144,000 Jewish converts to Christianity sealed for protection against the Wrath of God ehich are the 7 bowl judgments (Rev 15:1, Rev 15:7 and Rev 16:1). Why are they sealed? These 144,000 will live and inherit the land promised to Israel. They will populate the Promised Land during the 1000 year millennial kingdom.

Revelation 7:1-8
[1] And after these things I saw four angels standing on the four corners of the earth, holding the four winds of the earth, that the wind should not blow on the earth, nor on the sea, nor on any tree.
[2] And I saw another angel ascending from the east, having the seal of the living God: and he cried with a loud voice to the four angels, to whom it was given to hurt the earth and the sea,
[3] Saying, Hurt not the earth, neither the sea, nor the trees, till we have sealed the servants of our God in their foreheads.
[4] And I heard the number of them which were sealed: and there were sealed an hundred and forty and four

thousand of all the tribes of the children of Israel.
[5] Of the tribe of Juda were sealed twelve thousand. Of the tribe of Reuben were sealed twelve thousand. Of the tribe of Gad were sealed twelve thousand.
[6] Of the tribe of Aser were sealed twelve thousand. Of the tribe of Nepthalim were sealed twelve thousand. Of the tribe of Manasses were sealed twelve thousand.
[7] Of the tribe of Simeon were sealed twelve thousand. Of the tribe of Levi were sealed twelve thousand. Of the tribe of Issachar were sealed twelve thousand.
[8] Of the tribe of Zabulon were sealed twelve thousand. Of the tribe of Joseph were sealed twelve thousand. Of the tribe of Benjamin were sealed twelve thousand.

This fulfills the statement made by Christ in His Olivet Discourse:

> *And except those days should be shortened, there should   no flesh be saved: but for the elect's sake those days shall be shortened.*   Matthew 24:22

Finally, we should comment on what the designation of 144,000 actually represents. There are two points of view. The first proposes that the number 144,000 is not an actual number, and by association neither would be the 12,000 from each of 12 tribes of Israel. The second interpretation is to take these numbers literally. This author refuses to accept a purely symbolic use of 144,000 and 12,000. Why would a reasonable person believe anything else? If these numbers are symbolic, then why not make 1260 days symbolic, and every other number in the Book of Revelation? God does not cover up or distort facts. The 5th trumpet sounds.

Trumpet 5 (Woe 1)   Chapters 10, 11 & 23

The 5th trumpet is called *Woe 1*, and when it sounds, the *bottomless pit* is opened and an army of demons called *locusts* are released to torture mankind. The leader of this demonic force is a powerful fallen angel called *Abaddon*.

Revelation 9:1-12

*[1] And the **fifth angel sounded**, and I saw a star fall from heaven unto the earth: and to him was given the key of the bottomless pit.*

[2] And he opened the bottomless pit; and there arose a smoke out of the pit, as the smoke of a great furnace; and the sun and the air were darkened by reason of the smoke of the pit.

[3] And there came out of the smoke locusts upon the earth: and unto them was given power, as the scorpions of the earth have power.

[4] And it was commanded them that they should not hurt the grass of the earth, neither any green thing, neither any tree; but only those men which have not the seal of God in their foreheads.

[5] And to them it was given that they should not kill them, but that they should be tormented five months: and their torment was as the torment of a scorpion, when he striketh a man.

[6] And in those days shall men seek death, and shall not find it; and shall desire to die, and death shall flee from them.

[7] And the shapes of the locusts were like unto horses prepared unto battle; and on their heads were as it were crowns like gold, and their faces were as the faces of men.

[8] And they had hair as the hair of women, and their teeth were as the teeth of lions.

[9] And they had breastplates, as it were breastplates of iron; and the sound of their wings was as the sound of

chariots of many horses running to battle.
[10] And they had tails like unto scorpions, and there were stings in their tails: and their power was to hurt men five months.
[11] And they had a king over them, which is the angel of the bottomless pit, whose name in the Hebrew tongue is Abaddon, but in the Greek tongue hath his name Apollyon.
[12] One woe is past; and, behold, there come two woes more hereafter.

Trumpet 6 (Woe 2)

The 6th trumpet is Woe 2, and when sounded there are four angels loosed from their subterranean prison in the area of the Euphrates River where the Garden of Eden once stood. They kill by the use of smoke and brimstone which comes out of their mouth. Woe 1 only tormented mankind, but Woe 2 kills 1/3 of all mankind.

Revelation 9: 13-21
*[13] And the **sixth angel sounded**, and I heard a voice from the four horns of the golden altar which is before God,*
[14] Saying to the sixth angel which had the trumpet, Loose the four angels which are bound in the great river Euphrates.
[15] And the four angels were loosed, which were prepared for an hour, and a day, and a month, and a year, for to slay the third part of men.
[16] And the number of the army of the horsemen were two hundred thousand thousand: and I heard the number of them.
[17] And thus I saw the horses in the vision, and them that sat on them, having breastplates of fire, and of jacinth, and brimstone: and the heads of the horses were as the heads of lions; and out of their mouths issued fire and smoke and brimstone.

[18] By these three was the third part of men killed, by the fire, and by the smoke, and by the brimstone, which issued out of their mouths.
[19] For their power is in their mouth, and in their tails: for their tails were like unto serpents, and had heads, and with them they do hurt.
[20] And the rest of the men which were not killed by these plagues yet repented not of the works of their hands, that they should not worship devils, and idols of gold, and silver, and brass, and stone, and of wood: which neither can see, nor hear, nor walk:
[21] Neither repented they of their murders, nor of their sorceries, nor of their fornication, nor of their thefts.

Babylon is Destroyed   **Chapters 21 & 22**

It is not entirely clear when the city called Babylon (Revelation 17 and 18) will be destroyed, but it must be very near the end of Satan's reign over the earth.
Satan and his appointed henchmen (Antichrist and the False Prophet) have reigned over the earth for almost 1245 days. Satan has functioned as a King, and a king must have a kingdom. It appears that Satan will rebuild the ancient city of Babylon in Mesopotamia. This will be the seat of his political, social, economic and commercial powers. There is no doubt that during this period of time Satan will reside in a place called *Babylon*. It has been greatly disputed whether this is a city yet to be built, or an existing city which Satan will call *Babylon*.

Some have asserted that this Babylon is Rome…some Jerusalem…some even New York. It is really not worth being dogmatic over where Babylon will reside. It is important to realize that there will certainly be a place called *Babylon* which will be the city where Satan resides. First, recall that Satan is cast down to the earth in Revelation 12:7-9 Second, a seat of power in which Satan resides is not unique or new to the Tribulation period. When John wrote a letter to the Church at Satan dwelled in the town of Pergamum where the Church of Pergamum was located (Revelation 2:13).

The religious system which will rule over the world is portrayed to John as a *great whore* who offers herself to a sinful world. She is arrayed in beautiful scarlet and purple robes, adorned with gold and precious stones. However, her beauty and dress simply hide the apostasy that she represents. She is seen sitting upon a *beast* having *7 heads and 10 horns*. We immediately recognize this beast from Rev 13:1 as the *Antichrist*.

There is one other thing that reveals the true nature of this beautiful woman: she has on her forehead a name written, *MYSTERY, BABYLON THE GREAT, THE MOTHER OF HARLOTS AND ABOMINATIONS OF THE EARTH.*

Religious Babylon is Destroyed
Revelation 17:1-18

*[1] And there came **one of the seven angels which had the seven vials**, and talked with me, saying unto me, Come hither; I will shew unto thee the judgment of the great whore that sitteth upon many waters:*
[2] With whom the kings of the earth have committed fornication, and the inhabitants of the earth have been made drunk with the wine of her fornication.
[3] So he carried me away in the spirit into the wilderness: and I saw a woman sit upon a scarlet coloured beast, full of names of blasphemy, having seven heads and ten horns.
[4] And the woman was arrayed in purple and scarlet colour, and decked with gold and precious stones and pearls, having a golden cup in her hand full of abominations and filthiness of her fornication:
[5] And upon her forehead was a name written, MYSTERY, BABYLON THE GREAT, THE MOTHER OF HARLOTS

AND ABOMINATIONS OF THE EARTH.
[6] And I saw the woman drunken with the blood of the saints, and with the blood of the martyrs of Jesus: and when I saw her, I wondered with great admiration.
[7] And the angel said unto me, Wherefore didst thou marvel? I will tell thee the mystery of the woman, and of the beast that carrieth her, which hath the seven heads and ten horns.
[8] The beast that thou sawest was, and is not; and shall ascend out of the bottomless pit, and go into perdition: and they that dwell on the earth shall wonder, whose names were not written in the book of life from the foundation of the world, when they behold the beast that was, and is not, and yet is.
[9] And here is the mind which hath wisdom. The seven heads are seven mountains, on which the woman sitteth.
[10] And there are seven kings: five are fallen, and one is, and the other is not yet come; and when he cometh, he must continue a short space.
[11] And the beast that was, and is not, even he is the eighth, and is of the seven, and goeth into perdition.
[12] And the ten horns which thou sawest are ten kings, which have received no kingdom as yet; but receive power as kings one hour with the beast.
[13] These have one mind, and shall give their power and strength unto the beast.
[14] These shall make war with the Lamb, and the Lamb shall overcome them: for he is Lord of lords, and King of kings: and they that are with him are called, and chosen, and faithful.
[15] And he saith unto me, The waters which thou sawest, where the whore sitteth, are peoples, and multitudes, and nations, and tongues.
[16] And the ten horns which thou sawest upon the beast, these shall hate the whore, and shall make her desolate and naked, and shall eat her flesh, and burn her with fire.

[17] For God hath put in their hearts to fulfil his will, and to agree, and give their kingdom unto the beast, until the words of God shall be fulfilled.
[18] And the woman which thou sawest is that great city, which reigneth over the kings of the earth.

It is interesting to understand from Rev 17 who the Antichrist is and how he originated. Recall from Rev 13:1-10 that a great world leader who has assumed dictatorship over the entire world is *wounded to death,* but he rises and is taken over by Satan. Here we see a great *mystery* revealed to us.

- This *beast* is identical to that of Rev 13. His *power* is from the *dragon* (Satan). He is called the *antichrist*
- The beast supports both commercial and religious Babylon
- This *woman* is not a real whore, but represents the City of Babylon. In this city are found all types of Satanic worship, prostitution, pornography, sexual perversions and worldly desires come true.
- The beast (antichrist) is portrayed not as a normal man, but as a supernatural being. He is controlled by a demonic spirit who *was*: he existed before John. He is not: as John is being shown these future events in heaven, this demonic spirit is in a subterranean chamber called the *bottomless pit*. He will ascend up out of this pit to become the antichrist (Rev 11:7). He is destined to go into *perdition* (Rev 19:20).
- The beast has existed before and probably functioned as a demonic spirit controlling the King of one of the 5 kingdoms or empires (Rev 17:10). that preceded John's day and persecuted Israel (Egyptian, Assyrian, Babylonian, Medo-Persian and Grecian empires (Rev 17:10). The sixth empire was the Roman empire, and The seventh empire was Hitler's 3rd Reich. The 8th

world empire that will persecute and rule over Israel
is this beast! (Rev 17:11).

Commercial Babylon is Destroyed
The religious system that is centered in Babylon will be
world-wide and cause many worshippers to stumble and
fall. This religious system is surrounded by unprecedented
wealth and commercial systems. The merchants of the earth
worship money and economic power rather that Jesus
Christ. Both Timothy and Matthew warned us of the
dangers in worshipping earthly wealth.

> *For the love of money is the root of all evil: which while*
> *some coveted after, they have erred from the faith, and*
> *pierced themselves through with many sorrows.*
> I Tim 6:10

> *Do not store up for yourselves treasures on earth,*
> *where moths and vermin destroy, and where thieves*
> *break in and steal.*   Matthew 6:13

The City of Babylon will be destroyed by fire (Rev 18:8)
while the earth mourns. The merchants of Babylon will
weep from far off (Rev 18:15). Notice that Babylon is a
seaport city (Rev 18:17-19).

Revelation 18:1-24
[1] And after these things I saw another angel come down
from heaven, having great power; and the earth was
lightened with his glory.
[2] And he cried mightily with a strong voice, saying,
Babylon the great is fallen, is fallen, and is become the
habitation of devils, and the hold of every foul spirit, and a
cage of every unclean and hateful bird.
[3] For all nations have drunk of the wine of the wrath of
her fornication, and the kings of the earth have committed

fornication with her, and the merchants of the earth are waxed rich through the abundance of her delicacies.

[4] And I heard another voice from heaven, saying, Come out of her, my people, that ye be not partakers of her sins, and that ye receive not of her plagues.

[5] For her sins have reached unto heaven, and God hath remembered her iniquities.

[6] Reward her even as she rewarded you, and double unto her double according to her works: in the cup which she hath filled fill to her double.

[7] How much she hath glorified herself, and lived deliciously, so much torment and sorrow give her: for she saith in her heart, I sit a queen, and am no widow, and shall see no sorrow.

[8] Therefore shall her plagues come in one day, death, and mourning, and famine; and she shall be utterly burned with fire: for strong is the Lord God who judgeth her.

[9] And the kings of the earth, who have committed fornication and lived deliciously with her, shall bewail her, and lament for her, when they shall see the smoke of her burning,

[10] Standing afar off for the fear of her torment, saying, Alas, alas, that great city Babylon, that mighty city! for in one hour is thy judgment come.

[11] And the merchants of the earth shall weep and mourn over her; for no man buyeth their merchandise any more:

[12] The merchandise of gold, and silver, and precious stones, and of pearls, and fine linen, and purple, and silk, and scarlet, and all thyine wood, and all manner vessels of ivory, and all manner vessels of most precious wood, and of brass, and iron, and marble,

[13] And cinnamon, and odours, and ointments, and frankincense, and wine, and oil, and fine flour, and wheat, and beasts, and sheep, and horses, and chariots, and slaves, and souls of men.

[14] And the fruits that thy soul lusted after are departed

from thee, and all things which were dainty and goodly are departed from thee, and thou shalt find them no more at all.
[15] The merchants of these things, which were made rich by her, shall stand afar off for the fear of her torment, weeping and wailing,
[16] And saying, Alas, alas, that great city, that was clothed in fine linen, and purple, and scarlet, and decked with gold, and precious stones, and pearls!
[17] For in one hour so great riches is come to nought. And every shipmaster, and all the company in ships, and sailors, and as many as trade by sea, stood afar off,
[18] And cried when they saw the smoke of her burning, saying, What city is like unto this great city!
[19] And they cast dust on their heads, and cried, weeping and wailing, saying, Alas, alas, that great city, wherein were made rich all that had ships in the sea by reason of her costliness! for in one hour is she made desolate.
[20] Rejoice over her, thou heaven, and ye holy apostles and prophets; for God hath avenged you on her.
[21] And a mighty angel took up a stone like a great millstone, and cast it into the sea, saying, Thus with violence shall that great city Babylon be thrown down, and shall be found no more at all.
[22] And the voice of harpers, and musicians, and of pipers, and trumpeters, shall be heard no more at all in thee; and no craftsman, of whatsoever craft he be, shall be found any more in thee; and the sound of a millstone shall be heard no more at all in thee;
[23] And the light of a candle shall shine no more at all in thee; and the voice of the bridegroom and of the bride shall be heard no more at all in thee: for thy merchants were the great men of the earth; for by thy sorceries were all nations deceived.
[24] And in her was found the blood of prophets, and of saints, and of all that were slain upon the earth.

The Little Scroll   Chapter 12

The 7th Trumpet is about to sound, but before this happens John sees a *parenthetical vision*. In this vision, *another mighty angel* suddenly appears. He stands upon the earth with one foot in the sea and another on the land. In his *right hand is* a *little scroll*. John hears *seven thunders* speaking words, and as he is about to record their words he is told to *write them not*. The mighty angel standing upon the earth and the sea declares that all things on earth will be changed, and *time will be no longer*. The angel then declares that *in the days of the 7th trumpet, the mystery of God will be finished*. Since the 7th trumpet initiates the 7 Bowls of God's Wrath, It can be assumed that this little scroll contains a detailed record of what will happen to Satan and his followers after the church is raptured out. Strangely, John is told to *eat this scroll* and he does. The contents of the scroll caused his mouth to be *sweet as honey* but his *stomach bitter*. This sort of thing has happened before. When God called Ezekiel to speak to the lost house of Israel, he was given a *roll* (scroll) to eat which contained the message he was to preach. This message was *sweet to his mouth*.

Revelation 10:1-11
[1] And I saw another mighty angel come down from heaven, clothed with a cloud: and a rainbow was upon his head, and his face was as it were the sun, and his feet as pillars of fire:
[2] And he had in his hand a little book open: and he set his right foot upon the sea, and his left foot on the earth,
[3] And cried with a loud voice, as when a lion roareth: and when he had cried, seven thunders uttered their voices.
[4] And when the seven thunders had uttered their voices, I was about to write: and I heard a voice from heaven saying

unto me, Seal up those things which the seven thunders uttered, and write them not.

[5] And the angel which I saw stand upon the sea and upon the earth lifted up his hand to heaven,

[6] And sware by him that liveth for ever and ever, who created heaven, and the things that therein are, and the earth, and the things that therein are, and the sea, and the things which are therein, that there should be time no longer:

[7] But in the days of the voice of the seventh angel, when he shall begin to sound, the mystery of God should be finished, as he hath declared to his servants the prophets.

[8] And the voice which I heard from heaven spake unto me again, and said, Go and take the little book which is open in the hand of the angel which standeth upon the sea and upon the earth.

[9] And I went unto the angel, and said unto him, Give me the little book. And he said unto me, Take it, and eat it up; and it shall make thy belly bitter, but it shall be in thy mouth sweet as honey.

[10] And I took the little book out of the angel's hand, and ate it up; and it was in my mouth sweet as honey: and as soon as I had eaten it, my belly was bitter.

[11] And he said unto me, Thou must prophesy again before many peoples, and nations, and tongues, and kings.

Before we read about future things, we need to consider what will happen to the 2 witnesses that will prophesy in the Jerusalem temple as the 7 trumpets sound.

The Two Witnesses are Slain   Chapter 13

Previously, John the revelator was told about two witnesses and how they will testify over a 1260 day period of time. (Rev 11:3), he is now shown their fate. They will be killed by Satan and after 3.5 days of lying dead in the street they will be resurrected. Chronologically, their resurrection will likely immediately precede the sounding of the 7th trumpet. They will be resurrected with all the other dead in Christ at the *rapture*.

Revelation 11:7-12
[7] And when they shall have finished their testimony, the beast that ascendeth out of the bottomless pit shall make war against them, and shall overcome them, and kill them.
[8] And their dead bodies shall lie in the street of the great city, which spiritually is called Sodom and Egypt, where also our Lord was crucified.
[9] And they of the people and kindreds and tongues and nations shall see their dead bodies three days and an half, and shall not suffer their dead bodies to be put in graves.
[10] And they that dwell upon the earth shall rejoice over them, and make merry, and shall send gifts one to another; because these two prophets tormented them that dwelt on the earth.
[11] And after three days and an half the Spirit of life from God entered into them, and they stood upon their feet; and great fear fell upon them which saw them.
[12] And they heard a great voice from heaven saying unto them, Come up hither. And they ascended up to heaven in a cloud; and their enemies beheld them.

The two witnesses will finish their testimony of 1260 days, and then they will be killed. They will lie in a street of Jerusalem for 3.5 days, and then will be resurrected just before the 7th trumpet sounds. Their resurrection will likely coincide with the *Rapture* of all the saints when the 7th trumpet sounds, although it could be a separate event. The scriptures are silent as to exactly when they are raised. Since Satan is given 1260 days to reign over the earth with the antichrist and the false Prophet, the testimony of the two witnesses will begin exactly 3.5 days before the Great War in the heavenlies takes place as described in Rev 12. When these two witnesses are resurrected, there is a great earthquake in Jerusalem which destroys 1/10 of the city.

Earthquake Destroys 1/10 of Jerusalem　**Chapter 23**

Immediately after the 3 witnesses are raised from the dead, there is an earthquake which rocks the City of Jerusalem. This earthquake destroys 1/0 of the city. We are not told how many people die in this earthquake. Since we assume that the 2 witnesses are probably raised with the rest of the righteous dead at the sounding of the 7th trumpet, it is likely that this earthquake is the one recorded in Revelation 11:19.

Revelation 11:13
[13]　And the same hour was there a great earthquake, and the tenth part of the city fell, and in the earthquake were slain of men seven thousand: and the remnant were affrighted, and gave glory to the God of heaven.

The 3rd Woe Comes Quickly　**Chapters 10 & 11**
As the 5th trumpet sounded, an army of demon locusts were brought out to torment mankind (Rev 9:3-6). The sounding of the 6th trumpet brought about widespread destruction and death by demon horsemen (Rev 9:11-21). The 5th Trumpet Judgment was called *Woe 1*. The 6th trumpet judgment was called *Woe 2; Woe 3* will now come quickly. Woe 3 will commence when the 7th trumpet sounds, and it will bring forth both the rapture of the *Ecclesia* and the *7 Bowls of God's Wrath*.

Revelation 11:14
　　[14] The second woe is past; and behold, the third woe
　　　　　　cometh quickly

The 7th Trumpet Sounds   Chapter 23

The 7th and last trumpet sounds, and the Rapture of the church saints will now take place. The dead in Christ will rise first, and then those who are still alive will be caught up into the air to meet Jesus Christ. This gathering of the saints is depicted as a *wheat harvest.*

The Wheat Harvest of All Believers   Chapter 20

During the 3.5 year ministry of Christ, He often spoke parables and taught using agricultural examples. The rapture or snatching away of all living believers is described in Rev 14:14-16 in agricultural terms. John saw a future vision immediately after the Antichrist and the False Prophet arose. This vision reflected the fact that Israel was an agricultural society that relied heavily upon the wheat harvest in both everyday life and in its religious ceremonies (Feast of Unleavened Bread, Feast of Firstfruits and Feast of Pentecost). John saw a vision in which all believers in Christ were likened to wheat and its final harvest. The precious *wheat crop* is all *believers*, and the *reaper* is *Jesus Christ*. He is seen sitting on a *cloud* holding a *sharp sickle* with which he *harvests the earth.*

Revelation 14:14-16
[14] And I looked, and behold a white cloud, and upon the cloud one sat like unto the Son of man, having on his head a golden crown, and in his hand a sharp sickle.
[15] And another angel came out of the temple, crying with a loud voice to him that sat on the cloud, Thrust in thy sickle, and reap: for the time is come for thee to reap; for the harvest of the earth is ripe.
[16] And he that sat on the cloud thrust in his sickle on the earth; and the earth was reaped.

Rapture of the Saints

The Rapture of the saints now takes place. According to Paul, the dead in Christ will rise first; followed by all of those who are alive and still remain. The saints will be taken to heaven where they will be judged for *rewards*, not *salvation*.

Revelation 11:15-19

[15] And the seventh angel sounded; and there were great voices in heaven, saying, The kingdoms of this world are become the kingdoms of our Lord, and of his Christ; and he shall reign for ever and ever.

[16] And the four and twenty elders, which sat before God on their seats, fell upon their faces, and worshipped God,

[17] Saying, We give thee thanks, O Lord God Almighty, which art, and wast, and art to come; because thou hast taken to thee thy great power, and hast reigned.

[18] And the nations were angry, and thy wrath is come, and the time of the dead, that they should be judged, and that thou shouldest give reward unto thy servants the prophets, and to the saints, and them that fear thy name, small and great; and shouldest destroy them which destroy the earth.

[19] And the temple of God was opened in heaven, and there was seen in his temple the ark of his testament: and there were lightnings, and voices, and thunderings, and an earthquake, and great hail.

The Saints in Heaven   **Chapter 16**

Before opening the 7th seal, the Apostle John was shown a great multitude standing before the throne of God and before Jesus Christ (Rev.7:9-17). Fundamental scriptural truth revealed in many places is that the saints, those who belong to Jesus Christ, will not be subjected to the *Wrath of God*. The Wrath of God is clearly revealed to be the 7 Bowl Judgments (Rev 14:19, Rev 15:1, Rev 16:1). Carefully examining this great multitude, there can be little doubt that this is none other than the raptured saints; dead and alive from all ages past. This is shown to John about 1260 days before when the rapture actually occurs. Perhaps this is shown to John at this point in time to comfort him and to reassure him that those who survive the Wrath of Satan, persevere and refuse the mark of the beast unspeakable rewards await them.

Revelation 7:9-17

[9] After this I beheld, and, lo, a great multitude, which no man could number, of all nations, and kindreds, and people, and tongues, stood before the throne, and before the Lamb, clothed with white robes, and palms in their hands;

[10] And cried with a loud voice, saying, Salvation to our God which sitteth upon the throne, and unto the Lamb.

[11] And all the angels stood round about the throne, and about the elders and the four beasts, and fell before the throne on their faces, and worshipped God,

[12] Saying, Amen: Blessing, and glory, and wisdom, and thanksgiving, and honour, and power, and might, be unto our God for ever and ever. Amen.

[13] And one of the elders answered, saying unto me, What are these which are arrayed in white robes? and whence came they?

[14] And I said unto him, Sir, thou knowest. And he said to me, These are they which came out of great tribulation, and have washed their robes, and made them white in the blood of the Lamb.

[15] Therefore are they before the throne of God, and serve him day and night in his temple: and he that sitteth on the throne shall dwell among them.

[16] They shall hunger no more, neither thirst any more; neither shall the sun light on them, nor any heat.

[17] For the Lamb which is in the midst of the throne shall

feed them, and shall lead them unto living fountains of waters: and God shall wipe away all tears from their eyes.

This great multitude can be none other than the every saint who has accepted Jesus Christ as their Lord and Savior. John is not told *when* this will take place; only that it *will* take place. A little detective work will reveal beyond any reasonable doubt that this must take place as the 7th and last trumpet is blown. In Revelation 7:9-17, we are shown a *multitude that no man could number* standing before the Throne of God and before the Lamb of God. These are from *all nations, kindreds, people and tongues.* They have *come out of great tribulation.* They are clothed with *white robes.* These are the saints who have been raptured and met Jesus Christ in the air. This must also occur before the *Wrath of God* and the tribulation period is over…. and it does! There can be no doubt if scripture is to be interpreted literally that the rapture of the Saints occurs at the blowing of the 7th trumpet (Rev 11:15-19).

Rapture of the *Ecclesia*: Exegesis

The long awaited *rapture of the saints* is a fulfillment of I Thessalonians 15:51-52 for the church age, but it also fulfills a prophecy given to the prophet Daniel over 3400 years ago.

> *[1] And at that time shall Michael stand up, the great prince which standeth for the children of thy people: and there shall be a time of trouble, such as never was since there was a nation even to that same time: and at that time thy people shall be delivered, every one that shall be found written in the book.*
> *[2] And many of them that sleep in the dust of the earth shall awake, some to everlasting life, and some to shame and everlasting contempt.*
> *[3] And they that be wise shall shine as the brightness of*

71

the firmament; and they that turn many to righteousness as the stars forever and ever   Daniel 12:1-3

Carefully reviewing Hebrews Chapter 11, it is clear that the Old Testament believers were saved in the same way as New Testament believers. All are saved by *faith* in the Lord Jesus Christ. Over 400 Old Testament prophecies spoke of a *Messiah* that would arise who would save the Old Testament men and women of faith. New Covenant believers recognize this prophesied Messiah as our Lord Jesus Christ. Salvation and forgiveness of sin has always rested upon the same principle… salvation by faith. Those Old Testament believers who accepted Christ by faith are those revealed to Daniel in Dan 12:3a: *And many of them that sleep in the dust of the earth shall awake, some to everlasting life.*

In the Olivet Discourse, Christ spoke of how the earth would be harvested and how all believers would be gathered unto Him.

> *[29] Immediately after the tribulation of those days shall the sun be darkened, and the moon shall not give her light, and the stars shall fall from heaven, and the powers of the heavens shall be shaken:*
> *[30] And then shall appear the sign of the Son of man in heaven: and then shall all the tribes of the earth mourn, and they shall see the Son of man coming in the clouds of heaven with power and great glory.*
> *[31] And he shall send his angels with a great sound of a trumpet, and they shall gather together his elect from the four winds, from one end of heaven to the other.*   Matthew 24:29-31

The words of Christ in Matthew 24 are in exact agreement with the Revelation of the Prophet John in Revelation 11 and in Revelation 14.

Let us carefully note what Christ said in His own words; The sequence of events fits the end time events very well.

- Immediately *after* the tribulation of those days The sun and moon go dark, and stars fall from the heavens. This will happen when the 5th and 6th vial/bowl is poured out (Rev 16:10,18) as expected.
- Christ suddenly appears at His 2nd advent, and unlike the rapture of the saints; Everyone will see him coming
- Mat 24:31 actually precedes Mat 24:29-30 and is the rapture of the "elect"as the 7th trumpet sounds. This is not terribly unusual, since Woe 3 is the sounding of Trump 7 and it spawns or contains the 7 bowl judgments.
- The 7th trumpet brings forth two highly significant events: (1) Rapture of the church (alive) and resurrection of believers from all ages past (dead). (2) The 7th trumpet brings forth the *Wrath of God* which is identical to pouring out the *7 bowls or vials*.
- The word *rapture* does not appear in the Holy Scriptures. It is a word somewhat invented by all prophecy teachers. The term comes from a Latin word meaning *a carrying off, a transport, or a snatching away*. The concept of *carrying off* or the rapture of the church is clearly taught in Scripture. The rapture of the church is when Christ appears in the heavens and sends His angels to *harvest the earth*. The rapture is described by the apostle Paul in I Thessalonians 4:13–18 and I Corinthians 15:50–54. God will snatch away all living believers, and *resurrect* all believers who have died; giving both glorified and incorruptible bodies.

73

*For the Lord Himself will come down from heaven,
with a loud command, with the voice of the archangel
and with the trumpet call of God, and the dead in
Christ will rise first. After that, we who are still alive
and are left will be caught up together with them in
the clouds to meet the Lord in the air. And so we will
be with the Lord forever.*
I Thessalonians 4:16–17

The Rapture of saints at the 7th trumpet is a hotly contested conclusion. However, if the Holy Scriptures are carefully studied and analyzed it is obvious that there can be no other possible interpretation of Rev 11:15-19. Note what happens when the 7th trumpet sounds.

- The Kingdoms of this world have now become the Kingdoms of Christ and those who follow Him. Satan and his followers are about to experience the Wrath of God and then be destroyed at the Battle of Armageddon.
- The time has come for the dead and Christ and all the raptured saints (a) to be judged and (b) to be rewarded. This judgment is for rewards and not eternal life…. it is the Great Bema Seat Judgment in heaven and not on earth
- The time has come to destroy all of God's enemies on earth.

There is a promise to each Christian that no believer in Jesus Christ will have to experience the Wrath of God Romans 1:18, 5:9). The Wrath of God is clearly the 7 bowl judgments which immediately follow the last and 7th trumpet. Rapture of all living believers as the 7th trumpet sounds is totally consistent with what the Apostle Paul told the Christians at Corinth.

*[51] Behold, I shew you a mystery; We shall not all
sleep, but we shall all be changed,*

[52] In a moment, in the twinkling of an eye, at the last trump: for the trumpet shall sound, and the dead shall be raised incorruptible, and we shall be changed.
[53] For this corruptible must put on incorruption, and this mortal must put on immortality I Cor. 15:51-53

It also fulfills what Paul promised the church at Thessalonica (and us also).

[9] For God hath not appointed us to wrath, but to obtain salvation by our Lord Jesus Christ,
[10] Who died for us, that, whether we wake or sleep,we should live together with him I Thess. 5:9-10.

The Bema Seat Judgment   Chapter 28

Although not specifically stated in the Book of Revelation, the *Doctrine of Rewards* is clearly revealed in the holy Scriptures. Romans 14:10 says: *But why dost thou judge thy brother? or why dost thou set at nought thy brother? for we shall all stand before the judgment seat of Christ;* and in II Cor. 5:10: *For we must all appear before the judgment seat of Christ; that every one may receive the things done in his body, according to that he hath done, whether it be good or bad.* As soon as the rapture occurs, All saints alive and dead will stand before the Throne of God to receive rewards for how faithfully they have followed and served Jesus Christ (I Cor. 9:4-27, II Tim 2:5, Mat 28:18-20). This Judgment for rewards is called the *Bema Seat Judgment.*

Revelation 20:4-6
[4] And I saw thrones, and they sat upon them, and judgment was given unto them: and I saw the souls of them that were beheaded for the witness of Jesus, and for the word of God, and which had not worshipped the beast, neither his image, neither had received his mark upon their

*foreheads, or in their hands; and they lived and reigned
with Christ a thousand years.*
*[5] But the rest of the dead lived not again until the
thousand years were finished. This is the first resurrection.*
*[6] Blessed and holy is he that hath part in the first
resurrection: on such the second death hath no power, but
they shall be priests of God and of Christ, and shall reign
with him a thousand years.*

The Marriage of the Lamb   Chapters 24 & 25

The church of Jesus Christ is composed of all believers
dead or alive who have accepted Christ as the only Son of
God; believe that He was Crucified dead and buried; rose
again on the 3rd day; and ascended to heaven where He now
sits upon the right hand of God the Father. His sacrificial
death on the cross of Calvary and His atoning blood have
justified, glorified and sanctified all who believe upon His
name. The body of Christ is called the *Bride of Christ*
(Ephesians 5:22-32). After the rapture of the saints, alive
and dead, all will be given white robes of righteousness and
symbolically joined to Christ. The *marriage ceremony* will
take place in heaven before the 2nd advent of Christ and
the Battle of Armageddon (Revelation 19:7-9; 21:1-2). The
marriage Supper of the Lamb will take place on earth after
the Battle of Armageddon. It is proposed that it will take
place on the Feast of Tabernacles (Tishri 15-21).

Revelation 19:1-10
*[1] And after these things I heard a great voice of much
people in heaven, saying, Alleluia; Salvation, and glory,
and honour, and power, unto the Lord our God:*
*[2] For true and righteous are his judgments: for he hath
judged the great whore, which did corrupt the earth with
her fornication, and hath avenged the blood of his servants
at her hand.*

[3] And again they said, Alleluia. And her smoke rose up for ever and ever.

[4] And the four and twenty elders and the four beasts fell down and worshipped God that sat on the throne, saying, Amen; Alleluia.

[5] And a voice came out of the throne, saying, Praise our God, all ye his servants, and ye that fear him, both small and great.

[6] And I heard as it were the voice of a great multitude, and as the voice of many waters, and as the voice of mighty thunderings, saying, Alleluia: for the Lord God omnipotent reigneth.

[7] Let us be glad and rejoice, and give honour to him: for the marriage of the Lamb is come, and his wife hath made herself ready.

[8] And to her was granted that she should be arrayed in fine linen, clean and white: for the fine linen is the righteousness of saints.

[9] And he saith unto me, Write, Blessed are they which are called unto the marriage supper of the Lamb. And he saith unto me, These are the true sayings of God.

[10] And I fell at his feet to worship him. And he said unto me, See thou do it not: I am thy fellowservant, and of thy brethren that have the testimony of Jesus: worship God: for the testimony of Jesus is the spirit of prophecy.

Prelude to the 7 Bowl Judgments   Chapters 16 & 20

Having harvested all believers from the earth, God is now ready to pour out *His Wrath* upon Satan, the Antichrist, the False Prophet and all nonbelievers. Before John sees these things unfolding, he is shown all of those who have overcome Satan and have refused the mark of the Beast standing before the Throne of God in heaven. They are before the throne of God singing a *song* of victory.

Revelation 15:1-8

[1] And I saw another sign in heaven, great and marvelous, seven angels having the seven last plagues; for in them is filled up the Wrath of God.

[2] And I saw as it were a sea of glass mingled with fire: and them that had gotten the victory over the beast, and over his image, and over his mark, and over the number of his name, stand on the sea of glass, having the harps of God.

[3] And they sing the song of Moses the servant of God, and the song of the Lamb, saying, Great and marvellous are thy works, Lord God Almighty; just and true are thy ways, thou King of saints.

[4] Who shall not fear thee, O Lord, and glorify thy name? for thou only art holy: for all nations shall come and worship before thee; for thy judgments are made manifest.

[5] And after that I looked, and, behold, the temple of the tabernacle of the testimony in heaven was opened:

[6] And the seven angels came out of the temple, having the seven plagues, clothed in pure and white linen, and having their breasts girded with golden girdles.

[7] And one of the four beasts gave unto the seven angels seven golden vials full of the wrath of God, who liveth for ever and ever.

[8] And the temple was filled with smoke from the glory of God, and from his power; and no man was able to enter into the temple, till the seven plagues of the seven angels were fulfilled.

The 7 Bowl Judgments
The *Wrath of God*

Chapters 10 & 11

The 7 Bowl Judgments: *The Wrath of God*

Seven angels proceed from the throne room of God, each holding a *golden bowl*. Each is told in turn to pour his Bowl of God's Wrath upon earth and all who dwell therein.

The First 5 Bowl Judgments

The first 5 bowl judgments are devastating. The only people remaining upon the earth are unbelievers. Bowl 1 causes grievous sores to fall upon all those who have worshipped the beast and taken his mark upon their forehead or hand. Bowl 2 will turn the seas and oceans into blood and kill every creature in those waters. Bowl 3 will turn all fresh water into blood. No living animal or man can last very long without water. The 4th bowl will burn all men with fire and the 5th bowl will plunge the earth into darkness. Loel predicted over 2500 years ago that this would happen before Christ return

> *[11] Assemble yourselves, and come, all ye heathen, and gather yourselves together round about: thither cause thy mighty ones to come down, O LORD.*
> *[12] Let the heathen be wakened, and come up to the valley of Jehoshaphat: for there will I sit to judge all the heathen round about.*
> *[13] Put ye in the sickle, for the harvest is ripe: come, get you down; for the press is full, the fats overflow; for their wickedness is great.*
> *[14] Multitudes, multitudes in the valley of decision: for the day of the LORD is near in the valley of decision.*
> *[15] The sun and the moon shall be darkened, and the stars shall withdraw their shining.*

Joel 3:11-15

Revelation 16:1-11

[1] And I heard a great voice out of the temple saying to the seven angels, Go your ways, and pour out the vials of the wrath of God upon the earth.

*[2] And the **first** went, and **poured out his vial** upon the earth; and there fell a noisome and grievous sore upon the men which had the mark of the beast, and upon them which worshipped his image.*

*[3] And the **second** angel **poured out his vial** upon the sea; and it became as the blood of a dead man: and every living soul died in the sea.*

*[4] And the **third** angel **poured out his vial** upon the rivers and fountains of waters; and they became blood.*

[5] And I heard the angel of the waters say, Thou art righteous, O Lord, which art, and wast, and shalt be, because thou hast judged thus.

[6] For they have shed the blood of saints and prophets, and thou hast given them blood to drink; for they are worthy.

[7] And I heard another out of the altar say, Even so, Lord God Almighty, true and righteous are thy judgments.

*[8] And the **fourth** angel **poured out his vial** upon the sun; and power was given unto him to scorch men with fire.*

[9] And men were scorched with great heat, and blasphemed the name of God, which hath power over these plagues: and they repented not to give him glory.

*[10] And the **fifth** angel **poured out his vial** upon the seat of the beast; and his kingdom was full of darkness; and they gnawed their tongues for pain,*

[11] And blasphemed the God of heaven because of their pains and their sores, and repented not of their deeds.

The first 5 Bowl Judgments are severe and terrible. It is important to realize that these judgments are not poured out upon the earth over an extended period of time. *Bowl 1*: Horrible grievous sores fall on all unbelievers. *Bowl 2*: All sea creatures die. *Bowl 3*: All fresh water turns to blood. *Bowl 4*: Men are burned with fire from heaven. *Bowl 5*: Darkness descends upon the Satan's Kingdom. With all fresh water gone, mankind and all animals would last only a matter of days. It is shown in **Revelation**: *Mysteries Revealed* (Phillips) that the bowls are poured out between the rapture on The Feast of Trumpets (Tishri 1) and the Battle of Armageddon (Tishri 10)... a period of only 10 days. The Jews call this period the *Days of Awe*...It is the last period of time that all Jews can repent of their sins and be kept in the Book of Life for another year!

The 6th Bowl Judgment:
The 2nd Jerusalem Campaign

When the 6th bowl is poured out, God supernaturally creates an easy path for the armies of Satan to use as they march into Israel. The great *River Euphrates* is dried up so that armies from the east might advance against Jerusalem. The River Euphrates was near the Garden of Eden, and is often mentioned in scripture. Many times in the past, invading armies have come from the North; travelling just east of the Mediterranean Sea. This is the easiest way to approach Jerusalem, and was the same route followed by Nebuchadnezzar when the Babylonians completely destroyed Jerusalem and deported all the men and women of Israel for 70 years in the Babylonian empire. The purpose is to assemble all of Satan's followers for the *Battle of Armageddon* (Rev 12:16).

Revelation 16:12-16
*[12] And the **sixth** angel **poured out his vial** upon the great river Euphrates; and the water thereof was dried up, that the way of the kings of the east might be prepared.*
[13] And I saw three unclean spirits like frogs come out of the mouth of the dragon, and out of the mouth of the beast, and out of the mouth of the false prophet.

[14] For they are the spirits of devils, working miracles, which go forth unto the kings of the earth and of the whole world, to gather them to the battle of that great day of God Almighty.
[15] Behold, I come as a thief. Blessed is he that watcheth, and keepeth his garments, lest he walk naked, and they see his shame.
[16] And he gathered them together into a place called in the Hebrew tongue Armageddon.

Harvest of the Earth:
   The Grape Harvest of All Nonbelievers   **Chapter 20**

Following Bowl 6, there are two monumental events which will take place: (1) Satan and all of his followers will be gathered to a place called Armageddon (2) The 2nd Advent of Christ will take place.

Armageddon is generally believed to be on the Plains of Esmeralda just outside of Jerusalem. The purpose of this gathering depends upon the viewpoint. *Satan* will gather all of his forces to Jerusalem where he intends to completely destroy the Holy City and annihilate as many Jews as possible. *God* causes this to happen so that His Son Jesus Christ can completely destroy Satan and his forces at what is called the *Second Advent of Christ*. The second advent of Christ and his destruction of Satan is called the *Battle of Armageddon*. Before this great battle, all of Satan's followers will be supernaturally called to their final destruction. We previously discussed a vision in which John saw the saints being harvested as wheat to heaven. This vision corresponded to the rapture of all *believers* described in Rev 11:15-19 as the 7th trumpet sounded. John then saw a vision of what would happen to all *nonbelievers* at the end of the age. This vision was also based upon agricultural principles. In Revelation 14:14-16 Christ was depicted holding a *sharp sickle* with which one of His angels *harvests the earth.* The *fruit is ripe…* the time had come to harvest all living believers and resurrect all those dead in Christ. … This was the *Rapture* of the saints. The time has now come to harvest all unbelievers from the 4 corners of the earth and bring them to the Battle of Armageddon.

Revelation 14:17-19
[17] And another angel came out of the temple which is in heaven, he also having a sharp sickle.
[18] And another angel came out from the altar, which had power over fire; and cried with a loud cry to him that had the sharp sickle, saying, Thrust in thy sharp sickle, and gather the clusters of the vine of the earth; for her grapes are fully ripe.
[19] And the angel thrust in his sickle into the earth, and gathered the vine of the earth, and cast it into the great winepress of the wrath of God.

This vision was previously shown to John in Revelation 14:17-19 as part of the overview of the tribulation period when the 6 seals were broken and removed. That vision was a prediction and was clearly out of chronological sequence. Notice that John was allowed to see into the future 1260 days to a point in time *after* when the 6th bowl is poured out. This is the same literary structure previously used after the 6th seal was opened, and John saw the sealing of the 144,000 Jews against God's Wrath (7 Bowls) and the rapture of the saints as the 7th trumpet sounded.

The 7th Bowl Judgment

The *Wrath of God* has now come to its fullness as the 7th bowl is poured out. A great voice from the throne of God loudly proclaims: *It is done*! The heavens and earth are shaken and the City of Jerusalem is split into 3 parts (Rev 16: 18-19). All of the world's cities collapse and hail about the size of one talent (100 pounds) falls upon the earth; but iniquity will still abound and the followers of Satan refuse to repent (Rev 16:21). Note that in Rev 16:20 that *every island and every mountain on earth is not to be found.* Carefully note that this unprecedented and supernatural event was predicted as te 6th seal was broken by Jesus Christ. *This event cannot happen but one time in all of history, and it is proof that the 7 seals are not broken/removed over a period of time before the 7 trumpets sound and the 7 bowl judgments are poured out.* This truth cannot be seriously challenged or debunked if the Holy Scriptures are to be held as truth.

Revelation 16:17-21
[17] And the **seventh** *angel* **poured out his vial** *into the air; and there came a great voice out of the temple of heaven, from the throne, saying, It is done.*
[18] And there were voices, and thunders, and lightnings; and there was a great earthquake, such as was not since men were upon the earth, so mighty an earthquake, and so great.
[19] And the great city was divided into three parts, and the cities of the nations fell: and great Babylon came in remembrance before God, to give unto her the cup of the wine of the fierceness of his wrath.
[20] And every island fled away, and the mountains were not found.
[21] And there fell upon men a great hail out of heaven, every stone about the weight of a talent: and men

blasphemed God because of the plague of the hail; for the plague thereof was exceeding great.

The 2nd Advent of Christ   Chapter 26

The angels of the Lord have gathered Satan and all of his followers to the field of Armageddon. This we call this military campaign the *2nd Jerusalem Campaign*. Suddenly, **Christ appears in all of His resurrected glory**. Satan and all of his forces are quickly destroyed by a *sharp sword which comes out of the mouth of Christ*. The beast (antichrist) and the false prophet are thrown into the *Lake of Fire burning with brimstone.* Satan is cast into the *Bottomless Pit,* where he will kept for a thousand years as the Millennial Kingdom runs its course.

Revelation 19:11-16
[11]And I saw heaven opened, and behold a white horse; and he that sat upon him was called Faithful and True, and in righteousness he doth judge and make war.
[12] His eyes were as a flame of fire, and on his head were many crowns; and he had a name written, that no man knew, but he himself.
[13] And he was clothed with a vesture dipped in blood: and his name is called The Word of God.
[14] And the armies which were in heaven followed him upon white horses, clothed in fine linen, white and clean.
[15] And out of his mouth goeth a sharp sword, that with it he should smite the nations: and he shall rule them with a rod of iron: and he treadeth the winepress of the fierceness and wrath of Almighty God.
[16] And he hath on his vesture and on his thigh a name written, KING OF KINGS, AND LORD OF LORDS.

The Battle of Armageddon

The *1st Advent of Christ* was when he came as a suffering servant to fulfill the Law of Moses, offer himself as the perfect sacrifice for the sins of the world, and be resurrected into heaven. The *2nd Advent of Christ* is when he will appear as a Conquering King. He will destroy Satan and all of his army at the Great Battle of Armageddon. We call this the *2nd Jerusalem Campaign*.

Revelation 19:17-21

[17] And I saw an angel standing in the sun; and he cried with a loud voice, saying to all the fowls that fly in the midst of heaven, Come and gather yourselves together unto the supper of the great God;
[18] That ye may eat the flesh of kings, and the flesh of captains, and the flesh of mighty men, and the flesh of horses, and of them that sit on them, and the flesh of all men, both free and bond, both small and great.
[19] And I saw the beast, and the kings of the earth, and their armies, gathered together to make war against him that sat on the horse, and against his army.
[20] And the beast was taken, and with him the false prophet that wrought miracles before him, with which he deceived them that had received the mark of the beast, and them that worshipped his image. These both were cast alive into a lake of fire burning with brimstone.
[21] And the remnant were slain with the sword of him that sat upon the horse, which sword proceeded out of his mouth: and all the fowls were filled with their flesh

The Winepress of God   Chapter 20

In Revelation 14:14-19 we read where an angel was sitting upon a cloud with a sharp sickle in His hand. God sent an angel out of His temple and instructed the angel with the

sickle to *reap the earth,* for the *harvest of the earth is ripe.*
This harvest is the precious wheat; the elect of Jesus Christ;
and this harvest represents the *rapture* of the saints. In
Revelation 14:17-19, a third angel is seen with another
sharp sickle. A 4th angel emerges from the temple of God
and commanded the 3rd angel to reap the earth. This harvest
is of *grapes.* The grapes represent unbelievers who will be
gathered together (harvested) for the Battle of
Armageddon. This battle is symbolically called the
Winepress of God. Blood emerged from the *winepress,* and
it was so deep that it flowed unto the *bridles of the horses*
for *600 furlongs.* The carnage is so great that blood flowed
like water over 200 miles to a depth of about 4 feet.

Revelation 14:20
*[20] And the winepress was trodden without the city, and
blood came out of the winepress, even unto the horse
bridles, by the space of a thousand and six hundred
furlongs.*

**Fate of the Antichrist and
   The False Prophet   Chapters 26, 27 & 28**

We have already been told the fate of the Antichrist and the
False Prophet (Revelation 19:20). They are both cast into
the Lake of fire and Brimstone. Their source of power and
authority was that old dragon; Satan.

The Binding of Satan and the Millennial Kingdom

Satan will be held in the bottomless pit during the
millennial kingdom (1000 years). After that period of time
has run its course, Satan will be released for a *little season.*
After his (Satan) release, he will gather all sinners to one
final great confrontation outside of Jerusalem. As before,

the end is swift and complete. We call this the *3rd Jerusalem Campaign*. Satan is bound and cast into the Bottomless Pit, where he will remain for the 1000 year period called the *Millennial Kingdom*.

Revelation 20:1-3
[1] And I saw an angel come down from heaven, having the key of the bottomless pit and a great chain in his hand. [2] And he laid hold on the dragon, that old serpent, which is the Devil, and Satan, and bound him a thousand years, [3] And cast him into the bottomless pit, and shut him up, and set a seal upon him, that he should deceive the nations no more, till the thousand years should be fulfilled: and after that he must be loosed a little season.

Not much is given in the Book of Revelation about the 1000 year millennial kingdom. However, we know from the Old Testament that the 144,000 sealed Israelites and their offspring will live in the Promised Land to finally fulfill the *Abrahamic Covenant*.

Six times in Revelation 20:2-7, the millennial kingdom is specifically said to last 1000 years The millennial kingdom is undoubtedly the period of time in which God's chosen people (Israel) will finally inherit the land promised to both Moses and Joshua after the 40 year exodus from Egypt, and to Abraham when he was called by God. The Bible tells us that when Christ returns to the earth He will establish Himself as king in Jerusalem, sitting on the throne of David (Luke 1:32–33). The unconditional covenants demand a literal, physical return of Christ to establish the kingdom. The Abrahamic Covenant promised Israel a land, a posterity and ruler, and a spiritual blessing (Genesis 12:1–3). The Palestinian Covenant promised Israel a restoration to the land and occupation of the land (Deut. 30:1–10). The Davidic Covenant promised Israel a king from David's line who would rule forever, giving the nation rest from all their enemies (2 Samuel 7:10–13).

It is the fulfillment of many promises to the Nation of Israel, including that recorded by the prophet, Zachariah.

[8] In that day shall the LORD defend the inhabitants of Jerusalem; and he that is feeble among them at that day shall be as David; and the house of David shall be as God, as the angel of the LORD before them.
[9] And it shall come to pass in that day, that I will seek to destroy all the nations that come against Jerusalem.
[10] And I will pour upon the house of David, and upon the inhabitants of Jerusalem, the spirit of grace and of supplications: and they shall look upon me whom they have pierced, and they shall mourn for him   Zac 12:8-10

[6] And it shall come to pass in that day, that the light shall not be clear, nor dark:
[7] But it shall be one day which shall be known to the LORD, not day, nor night: but it shall come to pass, that at evening time it shall be light.
[8] And it shall be in that day, that living waters shall go out from Jerusalem; half of them toward the former sea, and half of them toward the hinder sea: in summer and in winter shall it be.
[9] And the LORD shall be king over all the earth: in that day shall there be one LORD, and his name one.
[10] All the land shall be turned as a plain from Geba to Rimmon south of Jerusalem: and it shall be lifted up, and inhabited in her place, from Benjamin's gate unto the place of the first gate, unto the corner gate, and from the tower of Hananeel unto the king's winepresses.
[11] And men shall dwell in it, and there shall be no more utter destruction; but Jerusalem shall be safely inhabited.
[12] And this shall be the plague wherewith the LORD will smite all the people that have fought against Jerusalem; Their flesh shall consume away while they

stand upon their feet, and their eyes shall consume away
in their holes, and their tongue shall consume away in
their mouth.   Zach 14:6-12

[25] And Judah and Israel dwelt safely, every man under
*his vine and under his **fig** tree, from Dan even to Beer-*
sheba, all the days of Solomon.   I Kings 4:25

Martyrs are Rewarded

It appears that those saints who were martyred during the
Great Tribulation will have a special reward: They will live
with Christ and reign with Him during the Millennial
Kingdom.

Revelation 20:4
[4] And I saw thrones, and they sat upon them, and
judgment was given unto them: and I saw the souls of them
that were beheaded for the witness of Jesus, and for the
word of God, and which had not worshipped the beast,
neither his image, neither had received his mark upon their
foreheads, or in their hands; and they lived and reigned
with Christ a thousand years.

End of the 1st Resurrection   Chapter 28

The 1st resurrection ends when the martyrs receive their
special rewards. Recall that they were seen waiting under
the throne of God (Rev 6:9-10) crying out for vengeance.
The 1st resurrection takes place over many thousands of
years.

Revelation 20:5-6
[5] But the rest of the dead lived not again until the
thousand years were finished. This is the first resurrection.
[6] Blessed and holy is he that hath part in the first

resurrection: on such the second death hath no power, but they shall be priests of God and of Christ, and shall reign with him a thousand years.

The End of Time as We Know It   Chapter 29

The Millennial Kingdom has come to an end. The Antichrist and the False Prophet were thrown into the Lake of Fire and Brimstone after the Battle of Armageddon. Satan was bound and cast into the *Bottomless Pit*, where he has remained for 1000 years until the Millennial Kingdom has come to an end. Satan is now released for a short time.

Revelation 20:7
[7] And when the thousand years are expired, Satan shall be loosed out of his prison.

Satan's Last Battle: *The 3rd Jerusalem Campaign*

After the 1000 year millennial kingdom is over, Satan will be loosed out of the bottomless pit. Satan goes out over all the earth, and gathers to him an army to challenge Jesus Christ one more time. Two things are obvious: First, Satan will never give up. Second, contrary to popular teaching there are evil people and unbelievers who have populated the millennial kingdom. Satan goes to the *four quarters of the earth* and marshals his forces once again outside of Jerusalem. We call this the *3rd Jerusalem Campaign*. It is believed that this is also the battle of Gog and Magog described by the prophet Ezekiel in Ezekiel 38-39.

As before, the end is quick and the victor is the same. Satan and his followers are *devoured with fire,* and Satan is cast into the Lake of Fire and Brimstone where he is tormented forever.

Revelation 20:8-10

[8] And shall go out to deceive the nations which are in the four quarters of the earth, Gog and Magog, to gather them together to battle: the number of whom is as the sand of the sea.

[9] And they went up on the breadth of the earth, and compassed the camp of the saints about, and the beloved city: and fire came down from God out of heaven, and devoured them.

[10] And the devil that deceived them was cast into the lake of fire and brimstone, where the beast and the false prophet are, and shall be tormented day and night forever and ever.

The White Throne Judgment   Chapter 28

The *Bema Seat Judgment* was held to reward all believers; the *White Throne Judgment* is to condemn all unbelievers and purge the earth of all sinners. This is the *second death*. It is said that *all believers only experience death once and all unbelievers experience death twice.* The second death is eternal separation from God.

The Great White Throne Judgment is a final judgment. All of the living followers of Satan have perished in the final battle. This judgment is for (1) Those that remain after the millennial kingdom and (2) all unbelievers. The earth, sea and hell (Gehenna) give up the dead in them and all are *judged according to their works.* Anyone whose name was not written in the *Book of Life* was cast into the *Lake of Fire.* Christ told John in Revelation The defeat of death and hell are the last foes to be conquered by Jesus Christ.

> *[26] The last enemy that shall be destroyed is*
> ***death.***   I Corinthians 15:26.

Revelation 20:11-15

[11] And I saw a great white throne, and him that sat on it, from whose face the earth and the heaven fled away; and

there was found no place for them.
[12] And I saw the dead, small and great, stand before
God; and the books were opened: and another book was
opened, which is the book of life: and the dead were judged
out of those things which were written in the books,
according to their works.
[13] And the sea gave up the dead which were in it; and
death and hell delivered up the dead which were in them:
and they were judged every man according to their works.
[14] And death and hell were cast into the lake of fire. This
is the second death.
[15] And whosoever was not found written in the book of
life was cast into the lake of fire.

New Heavens and a New Earth

God destroyed the earth by a great flood and promised
never to do this again by water. The earth will be destroyed
one more time to remove all sin from the earth.

Revelation 21:1
[1] And I saw a new heaven and a new earth: for the first
heaven and the first earth were passed away; and there was
no more sea.

The Eternal Kingdom of God Chapters 28 & 29

Following the Great White Throne judgment, Revelation
21:1 tells us that *I (John) saw a new heaven and a new*
earth: for the first heaven and the first earth had passed
away. In this new earth there are no more seas. John is next
shown the Holy City, the *New Jerusalem*, coming down
from heaven. The New Jerusalem is then described in great
detail. The narrative ends with the statement that no one

will dwell there except those whose names are written in a book called the *Lambs Book of Life.*

Revelation 21:2-8

[2] And I John saw the holy city, new Jerusalem, coming down from God out of heaven, prepared as a bride adorned for her husband.

[3] And I heard a great voice out of heaven saying, Behold, the tabernacle of God is with men, and he will dwell with them, and they shall be his people, and God himself shall be with them, and be their God.

[4] And God shall wipe away all tears from their eyes; and there shall be no more death, neither sorrow, nor crying, neither shall there be any more pain: for the former things are passed away.

[5] And he that sat upon the throne said, Behold, I make all things new. And he said unto me, Write: for these words are true and faithful.

[6] And he said unto me, It is done. I am Alpha and Omega, the beginning and the end. I will give unto him that is athirst of the fountain of the water of life freely.

[7] He that overcometh shall inherit all things; and I will be his God, and he shall be my son.

[8] But the fearful, and unbelieving, and the abominable, and murderers, and whoremongers, and sorcerers, and idolaters, and all liars, shall have their part in the lake which burneth with fire and brimstone: which is the second death.

The New Jerusalem   Chapter 29

Our Lord Jesus Christ has been resurrected from the grave, and He is preparing a place for us to live with Him throughout eternity.

*[2] In my Father's house are many mansions: if it were not so, I would have told you. I go to **prepare** a place for you.*   John 4:2

This place is called the *New Jerusalem*. The saints from all ages that have been resurrected and raptured will live in this magnificent structure during the 1000 year millennial kingdom. Its beauty cannot be described by mere words.

Revelation 21:9-27

[9] And there came unto me one of the seven angels which had the seven vials full of the seven last plagues, and talked with me, saying, Come hither, I will shew thee the bride, the Lamb's wife.
[10] And he carried me away in the spirit to a great and high mountain, and shewed me that great city, the holy Jerusalem, descending out of heaven from God,
[11] Having the glory of God: and her light was like unto a stone most precious, even like a jasper stone, clear as crystal;
[12] And had a wall great and high, and had twelve gates, and at the gates twelve angels, and names written thereon, which are the names of the twelve tribes of the children of Israel:
[13] On the east three gates; on the north three gates; on the south three gates; and on the west three gates.
[14] And the wall of the city had twelve foundations, and in them the names of the twelve apostles of the Lamb.
[15] And he that talked with me had a golden reed to measure the city, and the gates thereof, and the wall thereof.
[16] And the city lieth foursquare, and the length is as large as the breadth: and he measured the city with the reed, twelve thousand furlongs. The length and the breadth and the height of it are equal.
[17] And he measured the wall thereof, an hundred and forty and four cubits, according to the measure of a man, that is, of the angel.
[18] And the building of the wall of it was of jasper: and

the city was pure gold, like unto clear glass.

[19] And the foundations of the wall of the city were garnished with all manner of precious stones. The first foundation was jasper; the second, sapphire; the third, a chalcedony; the fourth, an emerald;

[20] The fifth, sardonyx; the sixth, sardius; the seventh, chrysolite; the eighth, beryl; the ninth, a topaz; the tenth, a chrysoprasus; the eleventh, a jacinth; the twelfth, an amethyst.

[21] And the twelve gates were twelve pearls; every several gate was of one pearl: and the street of the city was pure gold, as it were transparent glass.

[22] And I saw no temple therein: for the Lord God Almighty and the Lamb are the temple of it.

[23] And the city had no need of the sun, neither of the moon, to shine in it: for the glory of God did lighten it, and the Lamb is the light thereof.

[24] And the nations of them which are saved shall walk in the light of it: and the kings of the earth do bring their glory and honour into it.

[25] And the gates of it shall not be shut at all by day: for there shall be no night there.

[26] And they shall bring the glory and honour of the nations into it.

[27] And there shall in no wise enter into it any thing that defileth, neither whatsoever worketh abomination, or maketh a lie: but they which are written in the Lamb's book of life.

Gifts to the Resurrected Saints   Chapters 29 & 30

The resurrected saints will return to an Edenic state in which God will walk among them. A pure river clear as crystal will flow from the Throne of God, and on each side of the river there will be the *trees of life*. The earth and man is no longer cursed, and we will see His face. There will be no light in this new world except for the light which comes from the Lord God.

Revelation 22:1-5

[1] And he shewed me a pure river of water of life, clear as crystal, proceeding out of the throne of God and of the Lamb.
[2] In the midst of the street of it, and on either side of the river, was there the tree of life, which bare twelve manner of fruits, and yielded her fruit every month: and the leaves of the tree were for the healing of the nations.
[3] And there shall be no more curse: but the throne of God and of the Lamb shall be in it; and his servants shall serve him:
[4] And they shall see his face; and his name shall be in their foreheads.
[5] And there shall be no night there; and they need no candle, neither light of the sun; for the Lord God giveth them light: and they shall reign forever and ever

Words of Comfort and Warnings   Chapter 30

Chapter 22:6-20

[6]And he said unto me, These sayings are faithful and true: and the Lord God of the holy prophets sent his angel to shew unto his servants the things which must shortly be done.
[7] Behold, I come quickly: blessed is he that keepeth the sayings of the prophecy of this book.
[8] And I John saw these things, and heard them. And when I had heard and seen, I fell down to worship before the feet of the angel which shewed me these things.
[9] Then saith he unto me, See thou do it not: for I am thy fellowservant, and of thy brethren the prophets, and of them which keep the sayings of this book: worship God.

[10] And he saith unto me, Seal not the sayings of the prophecy of this book: for the time is at hand.

[11] He that is unjust, let him be unjust still: and he which is filthy, let him be filthy still: and he that is righteous, let him be righteous still: and he that is holy, let him be holy still.

[12] And, behold, I come quickly; and my reward is with me, to give every man according as his work shall be.

[13] I am Alpha and Omega, the beginning and the end, the first and the last.

[14] Blessed are they that do his commandments, that they may have right to the tree of life, and may enter in through the gates into the city.

[15] For without are dogs, and sorcerers, and whoremongers, and murderers, and idolaters, and whosoever loveth and maketh a lie.

[16] I Jesus have sent mine angel to testify unto you these things in the churches. I am the root and the offspring of David, and the bright and morning star.

[17] And the Spirit and the bride say, Come. And let him that heareth say, Come. And let him that is athirst come. And whosoever will, let him take the water of life freely.

[18] For I testify unto every man that heareth the words of the prophecy of this book, If any man shall add unto these things, God shall add unto him the plagues that are written in this book:

[19] And if any man shall take away from the words of the book of this prophecy, God shall take away his part out of the book of life, and out of the holy city, and from the things which are written in this book.

[20] He which testifieth these things saith, Surely I come quickly. Amen. Even so, come, Lord Jesus.

[21] The Grace of our Lord Jesus Christ be with you all, Amen

The Book of Revelation
In
Chronological Order
Scriptural Record

We will now present the Revelation Record from the King James Bible in the Chronological sequence that it occurs, with no comments. These scriptures are in the same order, and use the same headings, as those previously given with comments.

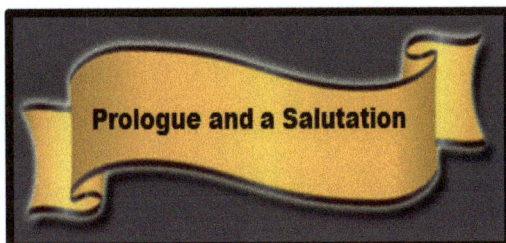

Prologue and a Salutation

Prologue and a Salutation

Revelation 1:1-8
[1] The Revelation of Jesus Christ, which God gave unto him, to shew unto his servants things which must shortly come to pass; and he sent and signified it by his angel unto his servant John:
[2] Who bare record of the word of God, and of the testimony of Jesus Christ, and of all things that he saw.
[3] Blessed is he that readeth, and they that hear the words of this prophecy, and keep those things which are written therein: for the time is at hand.

[4] John to the seven churches which are in Asia: Grace be unto you, and peace, from him which is, and which was, and which is to come; and from the seven Spirits which are before his throne;

[5] And from Jesus Christ, who is the faithful witness, and the first begotten of the dead, and the prince of the kings of the earth. Unto him that loved us, and washed us from our sins in his own blood,

[6] And hath made us kings and priests unto God and his Father; to him be glory and dominion for ever and ever. Amen.

[7] Behold, he cometh with clouds; and every eye shall see him, and they also which pierced him: and all kindreds of the earth shall wail because of him. Even so, Amen.

[8] I am Alpha and Omega, the beginning and the ending, saith the Lord, which is, and which was, and which is to come, the Almighty.

Instructions to John

Revelation 1:9-11
[9] I John, who also am your brother, and companion in tribulation, and in the kingdom and patience of Jesus Christ, was in the isle that is called Patmos, for the word of God, and for the testimony of Jesus Christ.

[10] I was in the Spirit on the Lord's day, and heard behind me a great voice, as of a trumpet,

[11] Saying, I am Alpha and Omega, the first and the last: and, What thou seest, write in a book, and send it unto the seven churches which are in Asia; unto Ephesus, and unto Smyrna, and unto Pergamos, and unto Thyatira, and unto Sardis, and unto Philadelphia, and unto Laodicea.

John Sees the Risen Christ

Revelation 1:12-16

[12] And I turned to see the voice that spake with me. And being turned, I saw seven golden candlesticks;
[13] And in the midst of the seven candlesticks one like unto the Son of man, clothed with a garment down to the foot, and girt about the paps with a golden girdle.
[14] His head and his hairs were white like wool, as white as snow; and his eyes were as a flame of fire; [15] And his feet like unto fine brass, as if they burned in a furnace; and his voice as the sound of many waters.
[16] And he had in his right hand seven stars: and out of his mouth went a sharp twoedged sword: and his countenance was as the sun shineth in his strength.

John's Reaction and the Sovereignty of Jesus Christ

Revelation 1: 17-20

[17] And when I saw him, I fell at his feet as dead. And he laid his right hand upon me, saying unto me, Fear not; I am the first and the last:
[18] I am he that liveth, and was dead; and, behold, I am alive for evermore, Amen; and have the keys of hell and of death.
[19] Write the things which thou hast seen, and the things which are, and the things which shall be hereafter;
[20] The mystery of the seven stars which thou sawest in my right hand, and the seven golden candlesticks. The seven stars are the angels of the seven churches: and the seven candlesticks which thou sawest are the seven churches.

Letters to the 7 Churches

Revelation 2:1-29

*[1] Unto the angel of the church of **Ephesus** write; These things saith he that holdeth the seven stars in his right hand, who walketh in the midst of the seven golden candlesticks;*

[2] I know thy works, and thy labour, and thy patience, and how thou canst not bear them which are evil: and thou hast tried them which say they are apostles, and are not, and hast found them liars:

[3] And hast borne, and hast patience, and for my name's sake hast laboured, and hast not fainted.

[4] Nevertheless I have somewhat against thee, because thou hast left thy first love.

[5] Remember therefore from whence thou art fallen, and repent, and do the first works; or else I will come unto thee quickly, and will remove thy candlestick out of his place, except thou repent.

[6] But this thou hast, that thou hatest the deeds of the Nicolaitans, which I also hate.

[7] He that hath an ear, let him hear what the Spirit saith unto the churches; To him that overcometh will I give to eat of the tree of life, which is in the midst of the paradise of God.

*[8] And unto the angel of the church in **Smyrna** write; These things saith the first and the last, which was dead, and is alive;*

[9] I know thy works, and tribulation, and poverty, (but thou art rich) and I know the blasphemy of them which say they are Jews, and are not, but are the synagogue of Satan.

[10] Fear none of those things which thou shalt suffer:

behold, the devil shall cast some of you into prison, that ye
may be tried; and ye shall have tribulation ten days: be
thou faithful unto death, and I will give thee a crown of life.
[11] He that hath an ear, let him hear what the Spirit saith
unto the churches; He that overcometh shall not be hurt of
the second death.

[12] And to the angel of the church in **Pergamos** write;
These things saith he which hath the sharp sword with two
edges;

[13] I know thy works, and where thou dwellest, even
where Satan's seat is: and thou holdest fast my name, and
hast not denied my faith, even in those days wherein
Antipas was my faithful martyr, who was slain among you,
where Satan dwelleth.

[14] But I have a few things against thee, because thou hast
there them that hold the doctrine of Balaam, who taught
Balac to cast a stumblingblock before the children of
Israel, to eat things sacrificed unto idols, and to commit
fornication.

[15] So hast thou also them that hold the doctrine of the
Nicolaitans, which thing I hate.

[16] Repent; or else I will come unto thee quickly, and will
fight against them with the sword of my mouth.

[17] He that hath an ear, let him hear what the Spirit saith
unto the churches; To him that overcometh will I give to eat
of the hidden manna, and will give him a white stone, and
in the stone a new name written, which no man knoweth
saving he that receiveth it.

[18] And unto the angel of the church in **Thyatira** write;
These things saith the Son of God, who hath his eyes like
unto a flame of fire, and his feet are like fine brass;

[19] I know thy works, and charity, and service, and faith,
and thy patience, and thy works; and the last to be more
than the first.

[20] Notwithstanding I have a few things against thee,
because thou sufferest that woman Jezebel, which calleth

herself a prophetess, to teach and to seduce my servants to commit fornication, and to eat things sacrificed unto idols.
[21] And I gave her space to repent of her fornication; and she repented not.
[22] Behold, I will cast her into a bed, and them that commit adultery with her into great tribulation, except they repent of their deeds.
[23] And I will kill her children with death; and all the churches shall know that I am he which searcheth the reins and hearts: and I will give unto every one of you according to your works.
[24] But unto you I say, and unto the rest in Thyatira, as many as have not this doctrine, and which have not known the depths of Satan, as they speak; I will put upon you none other burden.
[25] But that which ye have already hold fast till I come.
[26] And he that overcometh, and keepeth my works unto the end, to him will I give power over the nations:
[27] And he shall rule them with a rod of iron; as the vessels of a potter shall they be broken to shivers: even as I received of my Father.
[28] And I will give him the morning star.
[29] He that hath an ear, let him hear what the Spirit saith unto the churches.

Revelation 3:1-22

*[1] And unto the angel of the church in **Sardis** write; These things saith he that hath the seven Spirits of God, and the seven stars; I know thy works, that thou hast a name that thou livest, and art dead.*
[2] Be watchful, and strengthen the things which remain, that are ready to die: for I have not found thy works perfect before God.
[3] Remember therefore how thou hast received and heard, and hold fast, and repent. If therefore thou shalt not watch,

I will come on thee as a thief, and thou shalt not know what hour I will come upon thee.

[4] Thou hast a few names even in Sardis which have not defiled their garments; and they shall walk with me in white: for they are worthy.

[5] He that overcometh, the same shall be clothed in white raiment; and I will not blot out his name out of the book of life, but I will confess his name before my Father, and before his angels.

[6] He that hath an ear, let him hear what the Spirit saith unto the churches.

*[7] And to the angel of the church in **Philadelphia** write; These things saith he that is holy, he that is true, he that hath the key of David, he that openeth, and no man shutteth; and shutteth, and no man openeth;*

[8] I know thy works: behold, I have set before thee an open door, and no man can shut it: for thou hast a little strength, and hast kept my word, and hast not denied my name.

[9] Behold, I will make them of the synagogue of Satan, which say they are Jews, and are not, but do lie; behold, I will make them to come and worship before thy feet, and to know that I have loved thee.

[10] Because thou hast kept the word of my patience, I also will keep thee from the hour of temptation, which shall come upon all the world, to try them that dwell upon the earth.

[11] Behold, I come quickly: hold that fast which thou hast, that no man take thy crown.

[12] Him that overcometh will I make a pillar in the temple of my God, and he shall go no more out: and I will write

upon him the name of my God, and the name of the city of my God, which is new Jerusalem, which cometh down out of heaven from my God: and I will write upon him my new name.

[13] He that hath an ear, let him hear what the Spirit saith unto the churches.

*[14] And unto the angel of the church of the **Laodiceans** write; These things saith the Amen, the faithful and true witness, the beginning of the creation of God;*

[15] I know thy works, that thou art neither cold nor hot: I would thou wert cold or hot.

[16] So then because thou art lukewarm, and neither cold nor hot, I will spue thee out of my mouth.

[17] Because thou sayest, I am rich, and increased with goods, and have need of nothing; and knowest not that thou art wretched, and miserable, and poor, and blind, and naked:

[18] I counsel thee to buy of me gold tried in the fire, that thou mayest be rich; and white raiment, that thou mayest be clothed, and that the shame of thy nakedness do not appear; and anoint thine eyes with eyesalve, that thou mayest see.

[19] As many as I love, I rebuke and chasten: be zealous therefore, and repent.

[20] Behold, I stand at the door, and knock: if any man hear my voice, and open the door, I will come in to him, and will sup with him, and he with me.

[21] To him that overcometh will I grant to sit with me in my throne, even as I also overcame, and am set down with my Father in his throne.

[22] He that hath an ear, let him hear what the Spirit saith unto the churches.

John is Called to Heaven

Revelation 4:1-2

[1] After this I looked, and, behold, a door was opened in heaven: and the first voice which I heard was as it were of a trumpet talking with me; which said, Come up hither, and I will shew thee things which must be hereafter.
[2] And immediately I was in the spirit: and, behold, a throne was set in heaven, and one sat on the throne.

The Throne of God

Revelation 4:3-11

[3] And he that sat was to look upon like a jasper and a sardine stone: and there was a rainbow round about the throne, in sight like unto an emerald.
[4] And round about the throne were four and twenty seats: and upon the seats I saw four and twenty elders sitting, clothed in white raiment; and they had on their heads crowns of gold.
[5] And out of the throne proceeded lightnings and thunderings and voices: and there were seven lamps of fire burning before the throne, which are the seven Spirits of God.
[6] And before the throne there was a sea of glass like unto crystal: and in the midst of the throne, and round about the throne, were four beasts full of eyes before and behind.
[7] And the first beast was like a lion, and the second beast like a calf, and the third beast had a face as a man, and the fourth beast was like a flying eagle.
[8] And the four beasts had each of them six wings about him; and they were full of eyes within: and they rest not day and night, saying, Holy, holy, holy, Lord God Almighty, which was, and is, and is to come.
[9] And when those beasts give glory and honour and thanks to him that sat on the throne, who liveth for ever and

ever,

[10] The four and twenty elders fall down before him that sat on the throne, and worship him that liveth for ever and ever, and cast their crowns before the throne, saying,

[11] Thou art worthy, O Lord, to receive glory and honour and power: for thou hast created all things, and for thy pleasure they are and were created.

The 7-Seal Scroll: Who is worthy to Open?

Revelation 5:1-14

[1] And I saw in the right hand of him that sat on the throne a book written within and on the backside, sealed with seven seals.

[2] And I saw a strong angel proclaiming with a loud voice, Who is worthy to open the book, and to loose the seals thereof?

[3] And no man in heaven, nor in earth, neither under the earth, was able to open the book, neither to look thereon.

[4] And I wept much, because no man was found worthy to open and to read the book, neither to look thereon.

[5] And one of the elders saith unto me, Weep not: behold, the Lion of the tribe of Juda, the Root of David, hath prevailed to open the book, and to loose the seven seals thereof.

[6] And I beheld, and, lo, in the midst of the throne and of the four beasts, and in the midst of the elders, stood a Lamb as it had been slain, having seven horns and seven eyes, which are the seven Spirits of God sent forth into all the earth.

[7] And he came and took the book out of the right hand of him that sat upon the throne.

[8] And when he had taken the book, the four beasts and four and twenty elders fell down before the Lamb, having every one of them harps, and golden vials full of odours, which are the prayers of saints.

[9] And they sung a new song, saying, Thou art worthy to take the book, and to open the seals thereof: for thou wast slain, and hast redeemed us to God by thy blood out of every kindred, and tongue, and people, and nation;
[10] And hast made us unto our God kings and priests: and we shall reign on the earth.
[11] And I beheld, and I heard the voice of many angels round about the throne and the beasts and the elders: and the number of them was ten thousand times ten thousand, and thousands of thousands;
[12] Saying with a loud voice, Worthy is the Lamb that was slain to receive power, and riches, and wisdom, and strength, and honour, and glory, and blessing.
[13] And every creature which is in heaven, and on the earth, and under the earth, and such as are in the sea, and all that are in them, heard I saying, Blessing, and honour, and glory, and power, be unto him that sitteth upon the throne, and unto the Lamb for ever and ever.
[14] And the four beasts said, Amen. And the four and twenty elders fell down and worshipped him that liveth for ever and ever.

" Things Which Will Be"

Tribulation Period Overview

Opening/Breaking the First 6 Seals
Seals 1-4: Four Horsemen of the Apocalypse

Revelation 6:1-8

*[1] And I saw when the Lamb opened **one of the seals**, and I heard, as it were the noise of thunder, one of the four beasts saying, Come and see.*

[2] And I saw, and behold a white horse: and he that sat on him had a bow; and a crown was given unto him: and he went forth conquering, and to conquer.

*[3] And when he had opened the **second seal**, I heard the second beast say, Come and see.*

[4] And there went out another horse that was red: and power was given to him that sat thereon to take peace from the earth, and that they should kill one another: and there was given unto him a great sword.

*[5] And when he had opened the **third seal**, I heard the third beast say, Come and see. And I beheld, and lo a black horse; and he that sat on him had a pair of balances in his hand.*

[6] And I heard a voice in the midst of the four beasts say, A measure of wheat for a penny, and three measures of barley for a penny; and see thou hurt not the oil and the wine.

*[7] And when he had opened the **fourth seal**, I heard the voice of the fourth beast say, Come and see.*

[8] And I looked, and behold a pale horse: and his name that sat on him was Death, and Hell followed with him. And power was given unto them over the fourth part of the earth, to kill with sword, and with hunger, and with death, and with the beasts of the earth.

Seal 5: Death of Martyrs

Revelation 6:9-11
*[9] And when he had opened the **fifth seal**, I saw under the altar the souls of them that were slain for the word of God, and for the testimony which they held:*
[10] And they cried with a loud voice, saying, How long, O Lord, holy and true, dost thou not judge and avenge our blood on them that dwell on the earth?
[11] And white robes were given unto every one of them; and it was said unto them, that they should rest yet for a little season, until their fellow servants also and their brethren, that should be killed as they were, should be fulfilled.

Seal 6: Earth and Heavens Disrupted

Revelation 6:12-17
*[12] And I beheld when he had opened the **sixth seal**, and, lo, there was a great earthquake; and the sun became black as sackcloth of hair, and the moon became as blood;*
[13] And the stars of heaven fell unto the earth, even as a fig tree casteth her untimely figs, when she is shaken of a mighty wind.
[14] And the heaven departed as a scroll when it is rolled together; and every mountain and island were moved out of their places.
[15] And the kings of the earth, and the great men, and the rich men, and the chief captains, and the mighty men, and every bondman, and every free man, hid themselves in the dens and in the rocks of the mountains;
[16] And said to the mountains and rocks, Fall on us, and hide us from the face of him that sitteth on the throne, and from the wrath of the Lamb:
[17] For the great day of his wrath is come; and who shall be able to stand?

Seal 7: Silence in Heaven
Revelation 8:1

[1] And when he had opened the seventh seal, there was silence in heaven about the space of half an hour.

War in the Heavenlies:
The Sun Clothed Woman and the Man Child

Revelation 12:1-8
[1] And there appeared a great wonder in heaven; a woman clothed with the sun, and the moon under her feet, and upon her head a crown of twelve stars:
[2] And she being with child cried, travailing in birth, and pained to be delivered.
[3] And there appeared another wonder in heaven; and behold a great red dragon, having seven heads and ten horns, and seven crowns upon his heads.
[4] And his tail drew the third part of the stars of heaven, and did cast them to the earth: and the dragon stood before the woman which was ready to be delivered, for to devour her child as soon as it was born.
[5] And she brought forth a man child, who was to rule all nations with a rod of iron: and her child was caught up unto God, and to his throne.
[6] And the woman fled into the wilderness, where she hath a place prepared of God, that they should feed her there a thousand two hundred and threescore days.
[7] And there was war in heaven: Michael and his angels fought against the dragon; and the dragon fought and his angels,

[8] And prevailed not; neither was their place found any more in heaven.

Satan and His Angels are Cast Down to the Earth

Revelation 12:9-12
[9] And the great dragon was cast out, that old serpent, called the Devil, and Satan, which deceiveth the whole world: he was cast out into the earth, and his angels were cast out with him.
[10] And I heard a loud voice saying in heaven, Now is come salvation, and strength, and the kingdom of our God, and the power of his Christ: for the accuser of our brethren is cast down, which accused them before our God day and night.
[11] And they overcame him by the blood of the Lamb, and by the word of their testimony; and they loved not their lives unto the death.
[12] Therefore rejoice, ye heavens, and ye that dwell in them. Woe to the inhabiters of the earth and of the seal for the devil is come down unto you, having great wrath, because he knoweth that he hath but a short time.

Satan Attacks Jerusalem:
The 1ˢᵗ Jerusalem Campaign

Revelation 12:13-17
[13] And when the dragon saw that he was cast unto the earth, he persecuted the woman which brought forth the man child.
[14] And to the woman were given two wings of a great eagle, that she might fly into the wilderness, into her place, where she is nourished for a time, and times, and half a time, from the face of the serpent.
[15] And the serpent cast out of his mouth water as a flood after the woman, that he might cause her to be carried

away of the flood.

[16] And the earth helped the woman, and the earth opened her mouth, and swallowed up the flood which the dragon cast out of his mouth.

[17] And the dragon was wroth with the woman, and went to make war with the remnant of her seed, which keep the commandments of God, and have the testimony of Jesus Christ.

Rise of the Antichrist

Revelation 13:1-10
[1] And I stood upon the sand of the sea, and saw a beast rise up out of the sea, having seven heads and ten horns, and upon his horns ten crowns, and upon his heads the name of blasphemy.

[2] And the beast which I saw was like unto a leopard, and his feet were as the feet of a bear, and his mouth as the mouth of a lion: and the dragon gave him his power, and his seat, and great authority.

[3] And I saw one of his heads as it were wounded to death; and his deadly wound was healed: and all the world wondered after the beast.

[4] And they worshipped the dragon which gave power unto the beast: and they worshipped the beast, saying, Who is like unto the beast? who is able to make war with him?

[5] And there was given unto him a mouth speaking great things and blasphemies; and power was given unto him to continue forty and two months.

[6] And he opened his mouth in blasphemy against God, to blaspheme his name, and his tabernacle, and them that dwell in heaven.

[7] And it was given unto him to make war with the saints, and to overcome them: and power was given him over all kindreds, and tongues, and nations.

[8] And all that dwell upon the earth shall worship him,

whose names are not written in the book of life of the Lamb slain from the foundation of the world.
[9] If any man have an ear, let him hear.
[10] He that leadeth into captivity shall go into captivity: he that killeth with the sword must be killed with the sword. Here is the patience and the faith of the saints.

Rise of the False Prophet

Revelation 13:11-15
[11] And I beheld another beast coming up out of the earth; and he had two horns like a lamb, and he spake as a dragon.
[12] And he exerciseth all the power of the first beast before him, and causeth the earth and them which dwell therein to worship the first beast, whose deadly wound was healed.
[13] And he doeth great wonders, so that he maketh fire come down from heaven on the earth in the sight of men,
[14] And deceiveth them that dwell on the earth by the means of those miracles which he had power to do in the sight of the beast; saying to them that dwell on the earth, that they should make an image to the beast, which had the wound by a sword, and did live.
[15] And he had power to give life unto the image of the beast, that the image of the beast should both speak, and cause that as many as would not worship the image of the beast should be killed.

Mark of the Beast (666)

Revelation 13:16-18
[16] And he causeth all, both small and great, rich and poor, free and bond, to receive a mark in their right hand, or in their foreheads:
[17] And that no man might buy or sell, save he that had the mark, or the name of the beast, or the number of his

name.
[18] Here is wisdom. Let him that hath understanding count the number of the beast: for it is the number of a man; and his number is Six hundred threescore and six.

The Man Child Identified

Revelation 14:1-5
[1] And I looked, and, lo, a Lamb stood on the mount Sion, and with him an hundred forty and four thousand, having his Father's name written in their foreheads.
[2] And I heard a voice from heaven, as the voice of many waters, and as the voice of a great thunder: and I heard the voice of harpers harping with their harps:
[3] And they sung as it were a new song before the throne, and before the four beasts, and the elders: and no man could learn that song but the hundred and forty and four thousand, which were redeemed from the earth.
[4] These are they which were not defiled with women; for they are virgins. These are they which follow the Lamb whithersoever he goeth. These were redeemed from among men, being the firstfruits unto God and to the Lamb.
[5] And in their mouth was found no guile: for they are without fault before the throne of God.

The Gospel is Preached Unto All the World

Revelation 14:6-7
[6] And I saw another angel fly in the midst of heaven, having the everlasting gospel to preach unto them that dwell on the earth, and to every nation, and kindred, and tongue, and people,
[7] Saying with a loud voice, Fear God, and give glory to him; for the hour of his judgment is come: and worship him that made heaven, and earth, and the sea, and the fountains of waters.

The Two Witnesses

Revelation 11:1-6

[1] And there was given me a reed like unto a rod: and the angel stood, saying, Rise, and measure the temple of God, and the altar, and them that worship therein.
[2] But the court which is without the temple leave out, and measure it not; for it is given unto the Gentiles: and the holy city shall they tread under foot forty and two months.
[3] And I will give power unto my two witnesses, and they shall prophesy a thousand two hundred and threescore days, clothed in sackcloth.
[4] These are the two olive trees, and the two candlesticks standing before the God of the earth.
[5] And if any man will hurt them, fire proceedeth out of their mouth, and devoureth their enemies: and if any man will hurt them, he must in this manner be killed.
[6] These have power to shut heaven, that it rain not in the days of their prophecy: and have power over waters to turn them to blood, and to smite the earth with all plagues, as often as they will.

An Announcement: The Fate of Babylon

Revelation 14:8

[8] And there followed another angel, saying, Babylon is fallen, is fallen, that great city, because she made all nations drink of the wine of the wrath of her fornication

Warning about the Mark of the Beast

Revelation 14:9-13

[9] And the third angel followed them, saying with a loud voice, If any man worship the beast and his image, and receive his mark in his forehead, or in his hand,
[10] The same shall drink of the wine of the wrath of God,

which is poured out without mixture into the cup of his indignation; and he shall be tormented with fire and brimstone in the presence of the holy angels, and in the presence of the Lamb:

[11] And the smoke of their torment ascendeth up for ever and ever: and they have no rest day nor night, who worship the beast and his image, and whosoever receiveth the mark of his name.

[12] Here is the patience of the saints: here are they that keep the commandments of God, and the faith of Jesus.

[13] And I heard a voice from heaven saying unto me, Write, Blessed are the dead which die in the Lord from henceforth: Yea, saith the Spirit, that they may rest from their labours; and their works do follow them.

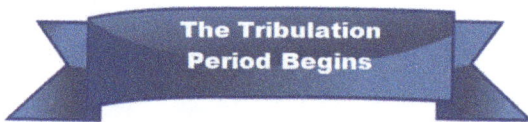

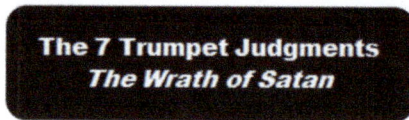

The Tribulation Period Begins

The 7 Trumpet Judgments
The Wrath of Satan

The First 4 Trumpet Judgments

Revelation 8:2-13

[2] And I saw the seven angels which stood before God; and to them were given **seven trumpets**.

[3] And another angel came and stood at the altar, having a golden censer; and there was given unto him much incense, that he should offer it with the prayers of all saints upon the golden altar which was before the throne.

[4] And the smoke of the incense, which came with the prayers of the saints, ascended up before God out of the angel's hand.

[5] And the angel took the censer, and filled it with fire of the altar, and cast it into the earth: and there were voices, and thunderings, and lightnings, and an earthquake.

[6] And the seven angels which had the seven trumpets prepared themselves to sound.

*[7] The **first angel sounded**, and there followed hail and fire mingled with blood, and they were cast upon the earth: and the third part of trees was burnt up, and all green grass was burnt up.*

*[8] And the **second angel sounded**, and as it were a great mountain burning with fire was cast into the sea: and the third part of the sea became blood;*

[9] And the third part of the creatures which were in the sea, and had life, died; and the third part of the ships were destroyed.

*[10] And the **third angel sounded**, and there fell a great star from heaven, burning as it were a lamp, and it fell upon the third part of the rivers, and upon the fountains of waters;*

[11] And the name of the star is called Wormwood: and the third part of the waters became wormwood; and many men died of the waters, because they were made bitter.

*[12] And the **fourth angel sounded**, and the third part of the sun was smitten, and the third part of the moon, and the third part of the stars; so as the third part of them was darkened, and the day shone not for a third part of it, and the night likewise.*

[13] And I beheld, and heard an angel flying through the midst of heaven, saying with a loud voice, Woe, woe, woe to the inhabiters of the earth by reason of the other voices of the trumpet of the three angels, which are yet to sound!

Sealing of the 144,000

Revelation 7:1-8
[1] And after these things I saw four angels standing on the four corners of the earth, holding the four winds of the earth, that the wind should not blow on the earth, nor on the sea, nor on any tree.
[2] And I saw another angel ascending from the east, having the seal of the living God: and he cried with a loud voice to the four angels, to whom it was given to hurt the earth and the sea,
[3] Saying, Hurt not the earth, neither the sea, nor the trees, till we have sealed the servants of our God in their foreheads.
[4] And I heard the number of them which were sealed: and there were sealed an hundred and forty and four thousand of all the tribes of the children of Israel.
[5] Of the tribe of Juda were sealed twelve thousand. Of the tribe of Reuben were sealed twelve thousand. Of the tribe of Gad were sealed twelve thousand.
[6] Of the tribe of Aser were sealed twelve thousand. Of the tribe of Nepthalim were sealed twelve thousand. Of the tribe of Manasses were sealed twelve thousand.
[7] Of the tribe of Simeon were sealed twelve thousand. Of the tribe of Levi were sealed twelve thousand. Of the tribe of Issachar were sealed twelve thousand.
[8] Of the tribe of Zabulon were sealed twelve thousand. Of the tribe of Joseph were sealed twelve thousand. Of the tribe of Benjamin were sealed twelve thousand.

The 5th Trumpet Sounds (Woe 1)

Revelation 9:1-12
*[1] And the **fifth angel sounded**, and I saw a star fall from heaven unto the earth: and to him was given the key of the bottomless pit.*

[2] And he opened the bottomless pit; and there arose a smoke out of the pit, as the smoke of a great furnace; and the sun and the air were darkened by reason of the smoke of the pit.

[3] And there came out of the smoke locusts upon the earth: and unto them was given power, as the scorpions of the earth have power.

[4] And it was commanded them that they should not hurt the grass of the earth, neither any green thing, neither any tree; but only those men which have not the seal of God in their foreheads.

[5] And to them it was given that they should not kill them, but that they should be tormented five months: and their torment was as the torment of a scorpion, when he striketh a man.

[6] And in those days shall men seek death, and shall not find it; and shall desire to die, and death shall flee from them.

[7] And the shapes of the locusts were like unto horses prepared unto battle; and on their heads were as it were crowns like gold, and their faces were as the faces of men.

[8] And they had hair as the hair of women, and their teeth were as the teeth of lions.

[9] And they had breastplates, as it were breastplates of iron; and the sound of their wings was as the sound of chariots of many horses running to battle.

[10] And they had tails like unto scorpions, and there were stings in their tails: and their power was to hurt men five months.

[11] And they had a king over them, which is the angel of the bottomless pit, whose name in the Hebrew tongue is Abaddon, but in the Greek tongue hath his name Apollyon.

[12] One woe is past; and, behold, there come two woes more hereafter.

The 6th Trumpet Sounds (Woe 2)

Revelation 9: 13-21

*[13] And the **sixth angel sounded**, and I heard a voice from the four horns of the golden altar which is before God,*

[14] Saying to the sixth angel which had the trumpet, Loose the four angels which are bound in the great river Euphrates.

[15] And the four angels were loosed, which were prepared for an hour, and a day, and a month, and a year, for to slay the third part of men.

[16] And the number of the army of the horsemen were two hundred thousand thousand: and I heard the number of them.

[17] And thus I saw the horses in the vision, and them that sat on them, having breastplates of fire, and of jacinth, and brimstone: and the heads of the horses were as the heads of lions; and out of their mouths issued fire and smoke and brimstone.

[18] By these three was the third part of men killed, by the fire, and by the smoke, and by the brimstone, which issued out of their mouths.

[19] For their power is in their mouth, and in their tails: for their tails were like unto serpents, and had heads, and with them they do hurt.

[20] And the rest of the men which were not killed by these plagues yet repented not of the works of their hands, that they should not worship devils, and idols of gold, and silver, and brass, and stone, and of wood: which neither can see, nor hear, nor walk:

[21] Neither repented they of their murders, nor of their sorceries, nor of their fornication, nor of their thefts.

Babylon is Destroyed

Revelation 14:8

[8] And there followed another angel, saying, Babylon is fallen, is fallen, that great city, because she made all nations drink of the wine of the wrath of her fornication.

Religious Babylon is Destroyed

Revelation 17:1-18

[1] And there came one of the seven angels which had the seven vials, and talked with me, saying unto me, Come hither; I will shew unto thee the judgment of the great whore that sitteth upon many waters:

[2] With whom the kings of the earth have committed fornication, and the inhabitants of the earth have been made drunk with the wine of her fornication.

[3] So he carried me away in the spirit into the wilderness: and I saw a woman sit upon a scarlet coloured beast, full of names of blasphemy, having seven heads and ten horns.

[4] And the woman was arrayed in purple and scarlet colour, and decked with gold and precious stones and pearls, having a golden cup in her hand full of abominations and filthiness of her fornication:

[5] And upon her forehead was a name written, MYSTERY, BABYLON THE GREAT, THE MOTHER OF HARLOTS AND ABOMINATIONS OF THE EARTH.

[6] And I saw the woman drunken with the blood of the saints, and with the blood of the martyrs of Jesus: and when I saw her, I wondered with great admiration.

[7] And the angel said unto me, Wherefore didst thou marvel? I will tell thee the mystery of the woman, and of the beast that carrieth her, which hath the seven heads and ten horns.

[8] The beast that thou sawest was, and is not; and shall ascend out of the bottomless pit, and go into perdition: and they that dwell on the earth shall wonder, whose names

were not written in the book of life from the foundation of the world, when they behold the beast that was, and is not, and yet is.

[9] And here is the mind which hath wisdom. The seven heads are seven mountains, on which the woman sitteth.

[10] And there are seven kings: five are fallen, and one is, and the other is not yet come; and when he cometh, he must continue a short space.

[11] And the beast that was, and is not, even he is the eighth, and is of the seven, and goeth into perdition.

[12] And the ten horns which thou sawest are ten kings, which have received no kingdom as yet; but receive power as kings one hour with the beast.

[13] These have one mind, and shall give their power and strength unto the beast.

[14] These shall make war with the Lamb, and the Lamb shall overcome them: for he is Lord of lords, and King of kings: and they that are with him are called, and chosen, and faithful.

[15] And he saith unto me, The waters which thou sawest, where the whore sitteth, are peoples, and multitudes, and nations, and tongues.

[16] And the ten horns which thou sawest upon the beast, these shall hate the whore, and shall make her desolate and naked, and shall eat her flesh, and burn her with fire.

[17] For God hath put in their hearts to fulfil his will, and to agree, and give their kingdom unto the beast, until the words of God shall be fulfilled.

[18] And the woman which thou sawest is that great city, which reigneth over the kings of the earth.

Commercial Babylon is Destroyed
Revelation 18:1-24

[1] And after these things I saw another angel come down from heaven, having great power; and the earth was lightened with his glory.

[2] And he cried mightily with a strong voice, saying, Babylon the great is fallen, is fallen, and is become the habitation of devils, and the hold of every foul spirit, and a cage of every unclean and hateful bird.

[3] For all nations have drunk of the wine of the wrath of her fornication, and the kings of the earth have committed fornication with her, and the merchants of the earth are waxed rich through the abundance of her delicacies.

[4] And I heard another voice from heaven, saying, Come out of her, my people, that ye be not partakers of her sins, and that ye receive not of her plagues.

[5] For her sins have reached unto heaven, and God hath remembered her iniquities.

[6] Reward her even as she rewarded you, and double unto her double according to her works: in the cup which she hath filled fill to her double.

[7] How much she hath glorified herself, and lived deliciously, so much torment and sorrow give her: for she saith in her heart, I sit a queen, and am no widow, and shall see no sorrow.

[8] Therefore shall her plagues come in one day, death, and mourning, and famine; and she shall be utterly burned with fire: for strong is the Lord God who judgeth her.

[9] And the kings of the earth, who have committed fornication and lived deliciously with her, shall bewail her, and lament for her, when they shall see the smoke of her burning,

[10] Standing afar off for the fear of her torment, saying, Alas, alas, that great city Babylon, that mighty city! for in one hour is thy judgment come.

[11] And the merchants of the earth shall weep and mourn over her; for no man buyeth their merchandise any more:

[12] The merchandise of gold, and silver, and precious stones, and of pearls, and fine linen, and purple, and silk, and scarlet, and all thyine wood, and all manner vessels of ivory, and all manner vessels of most precious wood, and of

brass, and iron, and marble,

[13] And cinnamon, and odours, and ointments, and frankincense, and wine, and oil, and fine flour, and wheat, and beasts, and sheep, and horses, and chariots, and slaves, and souls of men.

[14] And the fruits that thy soul lusted after are departed from thee, and all things which were dainty and goodly are departed from thee, and thou shalt find them no more at all.

[15] The merchants of these things, which were made rich by her, shall stand afar off for the fear of her torment, weeping and wailing,

[16] And saying, Alas, alas, that great city, that was clothed in fine linen, and purple, and scarlet, and decked with gold, and precious stones, and pearls!

[17] For in one hour so great riches is come to nought. And every shipmaster, and all the company in ships, and sailors, and as many as trade by sea, stood afar off,

[18] And cried when they saw the smoke of her burning, saying, What city is like unto this great city!

[19] And they cast dust on their heads, and cried, weeping and wailing, saying, Alas, alas, that great city, wherein were made rich all that had ships in the sea by reason of her costliness! for in one hour is she made desolate.

[20] Rejoice over her, thou heaven, and ye holy apostles and prophets; for God hath avenged you on her.

[21] And a mighty angel took up a stone like a great millstone, and cast it into the sea, saying, Thus with violence shall that great city Babylon be thrown down, and shall be found no more at all.

[22] And the voice of harpers, and musicians, and of pipers, and trumpeters, shall be heard no more at all in thee; and no craftsman, of whatsoever craft he be, shall be found any more in thee; and the sound of a millstone shall be heard no more at all in thee;

[23] And the light of a candle shall shine no more at all in thee; and the voice of the bridegroom and of the bride shall

be heard no more at all in thee: for thy merchants were the great men of the earth; for by thy sorceries were all nations deceived.

[24] And in her was found the blood of prophets, and of saints, and of all that were slain upon the earth.

The Little Scroll

Revelation 10:1-11

[1] And I saw another mighty angel come down from heaven, clothed with a cloud: and a rainbow was upon his head, and his face was as it were the sun, and his feet as pillars of fire:

[2] And he had in his hand a little book open: and he set his right foot upon the sea, and his left foot on the earth,

[3] And cried with a loud voice, as when a lion roareth: and when he had cried, seven thunders uttered their voices.

[4] And when the seven thunders had uttered their voices, I was about to write: and I heard a voice from heaven saying unto me, Seal up those things which the seven thunders uttered, and write them not.

[5] And the angel which I saw stand upon the sea and upon the earth lifted up his hand to heaven,

[6] And sware by him that liveth for ever and ever, who created heaven, and the things that therein are, and the earth, and the things that therein are, and the sea, and the things which are therein, that there should be time no longer:

[7] But in the days of the voice of the seventh angel, when he shall begin to sound, the mystery of God should be finished, as he hath declared to his servants the prophets.

[8] And the voice which I heard from heaven spake unto me again, and said, Go and take the little book which is open in the hand of the angel which standeth upon the sea and upon the earth.

[9] And I went unto the angel, and said unto him, Give me

the little book. And he said unto me, Take it, and eat it up; and it shall make thy belly bitter, but it shall be in thy mouth sweet as honey.

[10] And I took the little book out of the angel's hand, and ate it up; and it was in my mouth sweet as honey: and as soon as I had eaten it, my belly was bitter.

[11] And he said unto me, Thou must prophesy again before many peoples, and nations, and tongues, and kings.

The Two Witnesses are Slain

Revelation 11:7-12

[7] And when they shall have finished their testimony, the beast that ascendeth out of the bottomless pit shall make war against them, and shall overcome them, and kill them.

[8] And their dead bodies shall lie in the street of the great city, which spiritually is called Sodom and Egypt, where also our Lord was crucified.

[9] And they of the people and kindreds and tongues and nations shall see their dead bodies three days and an half, and shall not suffer their dead bodies to be put in graves.

[10] And they that dwell upon the earth shall rejoice over them, and make merry, and shall send gifts one to another; because these two prophets tormented them that dwelt on the earth.

[11] And after three days and an half the Spirit of life from God entered into them, and they stood upon their feet; and great fear fell upon them which saw them.

[12] And they heard a great voice from heaven saying unto them, Come up hither. And they ascended up to heaven in a cloud; and their enemies beheld them.

Earthquake Destroys 1/10 of Jerusalem

Revelation 11:13
[13] And the same hour was there a great earthquake, and the tenth part of the city fell, and in the earthquake were slain of men seven thousand: and the remnant were affrighted, and gave glory to the God of heaven.

The 3rd Woe Comes Quickly

Revelation 11:14
[14] The second woe is past; and behold, the third woe cometh quickly

The 7th Trumpet Sounds (Woe 3)

The Wheat Harvest of All Believers
Revelation 14:14-16
[14] And I looked, and behold a white cloud, and upon the cloud one sat like unto the Son of man, having on his head a golden crown, and in his hand a sharp sickle.
[15] And another angel came out of the temple, crying with a loud voice to him that sat on the cloud, Thrust in thy sickle, and reap: for the time is come for thee to reap; for the harvest of the earth is ripe.
[16] And he that sat on the cloud thrust in his sickle on the earth; and the earth was reaped.

Rapture of the Saints
Revelation 11:15-19
[15] And the seventh angel sounded; and there were great voices in heaven, saying, The kingdoms of this world are become the kingdoms of our Lord, and of his Christ; and he shall reign for ever and ever.
[16] And the four and twenty elders, which sat before God on their seats, fell upon their faces, and worshipped God,

[17] Saying, We give thee thanks, O Lord God Almighty, which art, and wast, and art to come; because thou hast taken to thee thy great power, and hast reigned.

[18] And the nations were angry, and thy wrath is come, and the time of the dead, that they should be judged, and that thou shouldest give reward unto thy servants the prophets, and to the saints, and them that fear thy name, small and great; and shouldest destroy them which destroy the earth.

[19] And the temple of God was opened in heaven, and there was seen in his temple the ark of his testament: and there were lightnings, and voices, and thunderings, and an earthquake, and great hail.

The Raptured and Dead Believers in Heaven
Revelation 7:9-17

[9]After this I beheld, and, lo, a great multitude, which no man could number, of all nations, and kindreds, and people, and tongues, stood before the throne, and before the Lamb, clothed with white robes, and palms in their hands;

[10] And cried with a loud voice, saying, Salvation to our God which sitteth upon the throne, and unto the Lamb.

[11] And all the angels stood round about the throne, and about the elders and the four beasts, and fell before the throne on their faces, and worshipped God,

[12] Saying, Amen: Blessing, and glory, and wisdom, and thanksgiving, and honour, and power, and might, be unto our God for ever and ever. Amen.

[13] And one of the elders answered, saying unto me, What are these which are arrayed in white robes? and whence came they?

[14] And I said unto him, Sir, thou knowest. And he said to me, These are they which came out of great tribulation, and have washed their robes, and made them white in the blood of the Lamb.

[15] Therefore are they before the throne of God, and serve him day and night in his temple: and he that sitteth on the throne shall dwell among them.
[16] They shall hunger no more, neither thirst any more; neither shall the sun light on them, nor any heat.
[17] For the Lamb which is in the midst of the throne shall feed them, and shall lead them unto living fountains of waters: and God shall wipe away all tears from their eyes.

The Bema Seat Judgment
Revelation 20:4-6

[4] And I saw thrones, and they sat upon them, and judgment was given unto them: and I saw the souls of them that were beheaded for the witness of Jesus, and for the word of God, and which had not worshipped the beast, neither his image, neither had received his mark upon their foreheads, or in their hands; and they lived and reigned with Christ a thousand years.
[5] But the rest of the dead lived not again until the thousand years were finished. This is the first resurrection.
[6] Blessed and holy is he that hath part in the first resurrection: on such the second death hath no power, but they shall be priests of God and of Christ, and shall reign with him a thousand years.

The Marriage of the Lamb
Revelation 19:1-10
[1] And after these things I heard a great voice of much people in heaven, saying, Alleluia; Salvation, and glory, and honour, and power, unto the Lord our God:
[2] For true and righteous are his judgments: for he hath judged the great whore, which did corrupt the earth with her fornication, and hath avenged the blood of his servants at her hand.
[3] And again they said, Alleluia. And her smoke rose up

for ever and ever.

[4] And the four and twenty elders and the four beasts fell down and worshipped God that sat on the throne, saying, Amen; Alleluia.

[5] And a voice came out of the throne, saying, Praise our God, all ye his servants, and ye that fear him, both small and great.

[6] And I heard as it were the voice of a great multitude, and as the voice of many waters, and as the voice of mighty thunderings, saying, Alleluia: for the Lord God omnipotent reigneth.

[7] Let us be glad and rejoice, and give honour to him: for the marriage of the Lamb is come, and his wife hath made herself ready.

[8] And to her was granted that she should be arrayed in fine linen, clean and white: for the fine linen is the righteousness of saints.

[9] And he saith unto me, Write, Blessed are they which are called unto the marriage supper of the Lamb. And he saith unto me, These are the true sayings of God.

[10] And I fell at his feet to worship him. And he said unto me, See thou do it not: I am thy fellowservant, and of thy brethren that have the testimony of Jesus: worship God: for the testimony of Jesus is the spirit of prophecy.

Prelude to the 7 Bowl/Vial judgments

Revelation 15:1-8

[1] And I saw another sign in heaven, great and marvelous, seven angels having the seven last plagues; for in them is filled up the Wrath of God.

[2] And I saw as it were a sea of glass mingled with fire: and them that had gotten the victory over the beast, and over his image, and over his mark, and over the number of his name, stand on the sea of glass, having the harps of God.

[3] And they sing the song of Moses the servant of God, and the song of the Lamb, saying, Great and marvellous are thy works, Lord God Almighty; just and true are thy ways, thou King of saints.

[4] Who shall not fear thee, O Lord, and glorify thy name? for thou only art holy: for all nations shall come and worship before thee; for thy judgments are made manifest.

[5] And after that I looked, and, behold, the temple of the tabernacle of the testimony in heaven was opened:

[6] And the seven angels came out of the temple, having the seven plagues, clothed in pure and white linen, and having their breasts girded with golden girdles.

[7] And one of the four beasts gave unto the seven angels seven golden vials full of the wrath of God, who liveth for ever and ever.

[8] And the temple was filled with smoke from the glory of God, and from his power; and no man was able to enter into the temple, till the seven plagues of the seven angels were fulfilled.

The 7 Bowl Judgments
The *Wrath of God*

The First 5 Bowl Judgments
Chapter 16:1-11

[1] And I heard a great voice out of the temple saying to the seven angels, Go your ways, and pour out the vials of the wrath of God upon the earth.

*[2] And the **first** went, and **poured out his vial** upon the earth; and there fell a noisome and grievous sore upon the men which had the mark of the beast, and upon them which worshipped his image.*

*[3] And the **second** angel **poured out his vial** upon the sea; and it became as the blood of a dead man: and every living soul died in the sea.*

*[4] And the **third** angel **poured out his vial** upon the rivers and fountains of waters; and they became blood.*

[5] And I heard the angel of the waters say, Thou art righteous, O Lord, which art, and wast, and shalt be, because thou hast judged thus.

[6] For they have shed the blood of saints and prophets, and thou hast given them blood to drink; for they are worthy.

[7] And I heard another out of the altar say, Even so, Lord God Almighty, true and righteous are thy judgments.

*[8] And the **fourth** angel **poured out his vial** upon the sun; and power was given unto him to scorch men with fire.*

[9] And men were scorched with great heat, and blasphemed the name of God, which hath power over these plagues: and they repented not to give him glory.

*[10] And the **fifth** angel **poured out his vial** upon the seat of the beast; and his kingdom was full of darkness; and they gnawed their tongues for pain,*

[11] And blasphemed the God of heaven because of their pains and their sores, and repented not of their deeds.

The 6ᵗʰ Bowl Judgment
Satan Prepares to Destroy Jerusalem:
 The 2ⁿᵈ Jerusalem Campaign

Revelation 16:12-16

*[12] And the **sixth** angel **poured out his vial** upon the great river Euphrates; and the water thereof was dried up, that the way of the kings of the east might be prepared.*

[13] And I saw three unclean spirits like frogs come out of the mouth of the dragon, and out of the mouth of the beast, and out of the mouth of the false prophet.

[14] For they are the spirits of devils, working miracles, which go forth unto the kings of the earth and of the whole world, to gather them to the battle of that great day of God Almighty.

[15] Behold, I come as a thief. Blessed is he that watcheth, and keepeth his garments, lest he walk naked, and they see his shame.

[16] And he gathered them together into a place called in the Hebrew tongue Armageddon.

Harvest of the Earth:
The Grape Harvest of All Unbelievers

Revelation 14:17-20
[17] And another angel came out of the temple which is in heaven, he also having a sharp sickle.

[18] And another angel came out from the altar, which had power over fire; and cried with a loud cry to him that had the sharp sickle, saying, Thrust in thy sharp sickle, and gather the clusters of the vine of the earth; for her grapes are fully ripe.

[19] And the angel thrust in his sickle into the earth, and gathered the vine of the earth, and cast it into the great winepress of the wrath of God.

The 7ᵗʰ Bowl Judgment

Revelation 16:17-21
[17] And the seventh angel poured out his vial into the air; and there came a great voice out of the temple of heaven, from the throne, saying, It is done.

[18] And there were voices, and thunders, and lightnings; and there was a great earthquake, such as was not since men were upon the earth, so mighty an earthquake, and so great.

[19] And the great city was divided into three parts, and

the cities of the nations fell: and great Babylon came in remembrance before God, to give unto her the cup of the wine of the fierceness of his wrath.

[20] And every island fled away, and the mountains were not found.

[21] And there fell upon men a great hail out of heaven, every stone about the weight of a talent: and men blasphemed God because of the plague of the hail; for the plague thereof was exceeding great.

The 2nd Advent of Christ

Revelation 19:11-16

[11]And I saw heaven opened, and behold a white horse; and he that sat upon him was called Faithful and True, and in righteousness he doth judge and make war.

[12] His eyes were as a flame of fire, and on his head were many crowns; and he had a name written, that no man knew, but he himself.

[13] And he was clothed with a vesture dipped in blood: and his name is called The Word of God.

[14] And the armies which were in heaven followed him upon white horses, clothed in fine linen, white and clean.

[15] And out of his mouth goeth a sharp sword, that with it he should smite the nations: and he shall rule them with a rod of iron: and he treadeth the winepress of the fierceness and wrath of Almighty God.

[16] And he hath on his vesture and on his thigh a name written, KING OF KINGS, AND LORD OF LORDS.

The Battle of Armageddon:
The 2nd Jerusalem Campaign

Revelation 19:17-21

[17] And I saw an angel standing in the sun; and he cried with a loud voice, saying to all the fowls that fly in the

midst of heaven, Come and gather yourselves together unto the supper of the great God;
[18] That ye may eat the flesh of kings, and the flesh of captains, and the flesh of mighty men, and the flesh of horses, and of them that sit on them, and the flesh of all men, both free and bond, both small and great.
[19] And I saw the beast, and the kings of the earth, and their armies, gathered together to make war against him that sat on the horse, and against his army.
[20] And the beast was taken, and with him the false prophet that wrought miracles before him, with which he deceived them that had received the mark of the beast, and them that worshipped his image. These both were cast alive into a lake of fire burning with brimstone.
[21] And the remnant were slain with the sword of him that sat upon the horse, which sword proceeded out of his mouth: and all the fowls were filled with their flesh

The Winepress of God

[20] And the winepress was trodden without the city, and blood came out of the winepress, even unto the horse bridles, by the space of a thousand and six hundred furlongs.

Satan is Bound for 1000 Years

Revelation 20:1-3
[1] And I saw an angel come down from heaven, having the key of the bottomless pit and a great chain in his hand.
[2] And he laid hold on the dragon, that old serpent, which is the Devil, and Satan, and bound him a thousand years,
[3] And cast him into the bottomless pit, and shut him up, and set a seal upon him, that he should deceive the nations no more, till the thousand years should be fulfilled: and after that he must be loosed a little season.

Martyrs are Rewarded

Revelation 20:4
[4] And I saw thrones, and they sat upon them, and judgment was given unto them: and I saw the souls of them that were beheaded for the witness of Jesus, and for the word of God, and which had not worshipped the beast, neither his image, neither had received his mark upon their foreheads, or in their hands; and they lived and reigned with Christ a thousand years.

End of the First Resurrection

Revelation 20:5-6
[5] But the rest of the dead lived not again until the thousand years were finished. This is the first resurrection. [6] Blessed and holy is he that hath part in the first resurrection: on such the second death hath no power, but they shall be priests of God and of Christ, and shall reign with him a thousand years.

Satan's Final Battle
The 3rd Jerusalem Campaign

Revelation 20:8-10
[8] And shall go out to deceive the nations which are in the four quarters of the earth, Gog and Magog, to gather them together to battle: the number of whom is as the sand of the sea.
[9] And they went up on the breadth of the earth, and compassed the camp of the saints about, and the beloved city: and fire came down from God out of heaven, and devoured them.
[10] And the devil that deceived them was cast into the lake of fire and brimstone, where the beast and the false prophet are, and shall be tormented day and night forever and ever.

The White Throne Judgment

Revelation 20:11-15
[11] And I saw a great white throne, and him that sat on it, from whose face the earth and the heaven fled away; and there was found no place for them.
[12] And I saw the dead, small and great, stand before God; and the books were opened: and another book was opened, which is the book of life: and the dead were judged out of those things which were written in the books, according to their works.
[13] And the sea gave up the dead which were in it; and death and hell delivered up the dead which were in them: and they were judged every man according to their works.
[14] And death and hell were cast into the lake of fire. This is the second death.
[15] And whosoever was not found written in the book of life was cast into the lake of fire. Revelation 20:11-15

New Heavens and a New Earth

Revelation 21:1
[1] And I saw a new heaven and a new earth: for the first heaven and the first earth were passed away; and there was no more sea.

The Eternal Kingdom of God

Revelation 21:2-8
[2] And I John saw the holy city, new Jerusalem, coming down from God out of heaven, prepared as a bride adorned for her husband.
[3] And I heard a great voice out of heaven saying, Behold, the tabernacle of God is with men, and he will dwell with them, and they shall be his people, and God himself shall

be with them, and be their God.

[4] And God shall wipe away all tears from their eyes; and there shall be no more death, neither sorrow, nor crying, neither shall there be any more pain: for the former things are passed away.

[5] And he that sat upon the throne said, Behold, I make all things new. And he said unto me, Write: for these words are true and faithful.

[6] And he said unto me, It is done. I am Alpha and Omega, the beginning and the end. I will give unto him that is athirst of the fountain of the water of life freely.

[7] He that overcometh shall inherit all things; and I will be his God, and he shall be my son.

[8] But the fearful, and unbelieving, and the abominable, and murderers, and whoremongers, and sorcerers, and idolaters, and all liars, shall have their part in the lake which burneth with fire and brimstone: which is the second death.

The New Jerusalem

Revelation 21:9-27

[9] And there came unto me one of the seven angels which had the seven vials full of the seven last plagues, and talked with me, saying, Come hither, I will shew thee the bride, the Lamb's wife.

[10] And he carried me away in the spirit to a great and high mountain, and shewed me that great city, the holy Jerusalem, descending out of heaven from God,

[11] Having the glory of God: and her light was like unto a stone most precious, even like a jasper stone, clear as crystal;

[12] And had a wall great and high, and had twelve gates, and at the gates twelve angels, and names written thereon, which are the names of the twelve tribes of the children of Israel:

[13] On the east three gates; on the north three gates; on the south three gates; and on the west three gates.

[14] And the wall of the city had twelve foundations, and in them the names of the twelve apostles of the Lamb.

[15] And he that talked with me had a golden reed to measure the city, and the gates thereof, and the wall thereof.

[16] And the city lieth foursquare, and the length is as large as the breadth: and he measured the city with the reed, twelve thousand furlongs. The length and the breadth and the height of it are equal.

[17] And he measured the wall thereof, an hundred and forty and four cubits, according to the measure of a man, that is, of the angel.

[18] And the building of the wall of it was of jasper: and the city was pure gold, like unto clear glass.

[19] And the foundations of the wall of the city were garnished with all manner of precious stones. The first foundation was jasper; the second, sapphire; the third, a chalcedony; the fourth, an emerald;

[20] The fifth, sardonyx; the sixth, sardius; the seventh, chrysolite; the eighth, beryl; the ninth, a topaz; the tenth, a chrysoprasus; the eleventh, a jacinth; the twelfth, an amethyst.

[21] And the twelve gates were twelve pearls; every several gate was of one pearl: and the street of the city was pure gold, as it were transparent glass.

[22] And I saw no temple therein: for the Lord God Almighty and the Lamb are the temple of it.

[23] And the city had no need of the sun, neither of the moon, to shine in it: for the glory of God did lighten it, and the Lamb is the light thereof.

[24] And the nations of them which are saved shall walk in the light of it: and the kings of the earth do bring their glory and honour into it.

[25] And the gates of it shall not be shut at all by day: for

there shall be no night there.

[26] And they shall bring the glory and honour of the nations into it.

[27] And there shall in no wise enter into it any thing that defileth, neither whatsoever worketh abomination, or maketh a lie: but they which are written in the Lamb's book of life.

Gifts to the Resurrected Saints

Revelation 22:1-5

[1] And he shewed me a pure river of water of life, clear as crystal, proceeding out of the throne of God and of the Lamb.

[2] In the midst of the street of it, and on either side of the river, was there the tree of life, which bare twelve manner of fruits, and yielded her fruit every month: and the leaves of the tree were for the healing of the nations.

[3] And there shall be no more curse: but the throne of God and of the Lamb shall be in it; and his servants shall serve him:

[4] And they shall see his face; and his name shall be in their foreheads.

[5] And there shall be no night there; and they need no candle, neither light of the sun; for the Lord God giveth them light: and they shall reign forever and ever

Words of Comfort and Warning

Chapter 22:6-20

[6]And he said unto me, These sayings are faithful and true: and the Lord God of the holy prophets sent his angel to shew unto his servants the things which must shortly be done.

[7] Behold, I come quickly: blessed is he that keepeth the

sayings of the prophecy of this book.

[8] And I John saw these things, and heard them. And when I had heard and seen, I fell down to worship before the feet of the angel which shewed me these things.

[9] Then saith he unto me, See thou do it not: for I am thy fellowservant, and of thy brethren the prophets, and of them which keep the sayings of this book: worship God.

[10] And he saith unto me, Seal not the sayings of the prophecy of this book: for the time is at hand.

[11] He that is unjust, let him be unjust still: and he which is filthy, let him be filthy still: and he that is righteous, let him be righteous still: and he that is holy, let him be holy still.

[12] And, behold, I come quickly; and my reward is with me, to give every man according as his work shall be.

[13] I am Alpha and Omega, the beginning and the end, the first and the last.

[14] Blessed are they that do his commandments, that they may have right to the tree of life, and may enter in through the gates into the city.

[15] For without are dogs, and sorcerers, and whoremongers, and murderers, and idolaters, and whosoever loveth and maketh a lie.

[16] I Jesus have sent mine angel to testify unto you these things in the churches. I am the root and the offspring of David, and the bright and morning star.

[17] And the Spirit and the bride say, Come. And let him that heareth say, Come. And let him that is athirst come. And whosoever will, let him take the water of life freely.

[18] For I testify unto every man that heareth the words of the prophecy of this book, If any man shall add unto these things, God shall add unto him the plagues that are written in this book:

[19] And if any man shall take away from the words of the book of this prophecy, God shall take away his part out of the book of life, and out of the holy city, and from the things

which are written in this book.
[20] He which testifieth these things saith, Surely I come quickly. Amen. Even so, come, Lord Jesus.

[21] The Grace of our Lord Jesus Christ be with you all,   Amen

Bibliography

1.0 Phillips, Don T., **Revelation:** *Mysteries Revealed,*
   2nd Edition, ISBN 978-1-62137-119-1,
   Virtualbookworm Publishing Company,
   http://www.amazon.com/The-Book-Revelation-
   Mysteries-Revealed/dp/16026488752012, 2012

2.0 Phillips, Don T., **A Sequential Chronology
   Of End Time Events:** *Condensed Edition,* ISBN
   978-1-62137-754-2, Virtualbookworm Publishing
   Company

www.ingramcontent.com/pod-product-compliance
Lightning Source LLC
Chambersburg PA
CBHW040418110426
42813CB00013B/2693